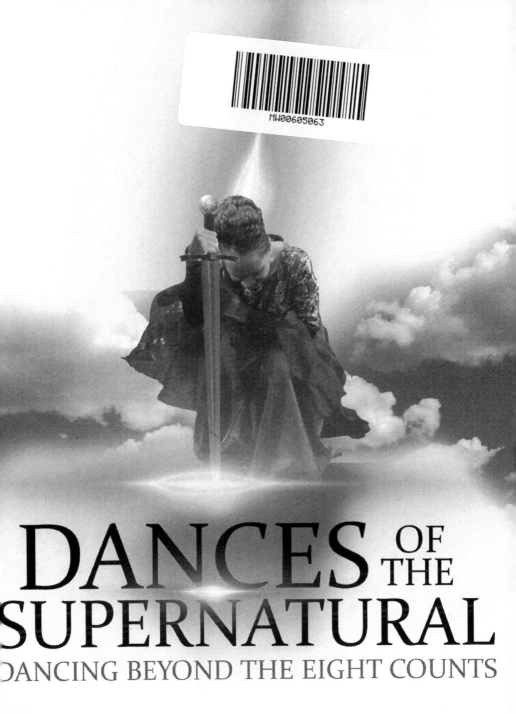

DANCES OF THE SUPERNATURAL

DANCING BEYOND THE EIGHT COUNTS

KATRINA R. CARTER

Katrina R. Carter
513-549-4509
www.HeavenlyDoveMinistries.org
heavenlydoveministries@gmail.com
214-326-5033 | www.eaglesiti.org

ISBN # 978-1-949826-13-5

Published by: EAGLES GLOBAL Publishing | Frisco, Texas
In conjunction with the 2019 Eagles Authors Course
Cover & interior designed by PublishAffordably.com | (773) 783-2981

DEDICATION

This book is dedicated to my Mom, Crystal "Byrd" Davis,

who is soaring in Heaven.

She always had the desire to write a book.

May your dream live on through me.

// KATRINA R. CARTER

ACKNOWLEDGMENTS

Thank you, Lord, for who You are in my life, and for restoring my voice. Our relationship has forever impacted me to live in the Supernatural.

To my husband, Lucien, our children, and my family. Thank you for believing in the God in me. You all keep me strong and balanced. Your support and sacrifice is greatly appreciated.

Much gratitude is extended to my spiritual parents, Drs. Pamela and Chris Hardy, Jerry Culbreth, and Gwendolyn Parrish. Your teaching, guidance, wisdom, and love have served as great encouragement through the years, especially during this writing process.

// KATRINA R. CARTER

CONTENTS

// KATRINA R. CARTER

INTRODUCTION

God is calling us to higher levels in our worship as a lifestyle. This call is also a call to function in the supernatural. God is restoring healing, deliverance, and miracles to the Church just as we saw in the Biblical days. We are instructed by Christ to go spread the gospel message to all. He was not specific in how we are to go, but Christ did say go. We each we were given gifts and we have been provided with the support of Heaven to follow us as we go.

My Encounter with dances of the supernatural:

In 2011, the Lord led me to visit a church in my hometown of Cincinnati, Ohio, just to rest and hide out. The pastors of this local fellowship asked me to minister a dance for their congregation. I had no dance garments with me, so their dancers allowed me to wear garments that they already had stored at the church.

Then one of the pastor's daughters came to me and said, "What song would you like to minister to?"

I felt the Spirit of God rise in me, and HE said, "I am here to serve. You may choose whatever song you desire."

She looked at me and said, "Wow. Ok."

I was invited to minister just before the preached word. When she told me the song, I was thankful because it was a song that I was familiar with. The song started, and the dance began, but then something peculiar happened to me. It seemed as if Katrina was no longer present. I wasn't dancing anymore, the Lord led me to lay hands, prophesy, and cast out demons.

I remember sitting on the floor at the altar, crying, and I heard the cries of others in the room who had received healing. Then the pastor walked to the podium and said to the congregation, "The Spirit of the Lord has moved. There is no need to preach."

Then those who still needed prayer were prayed for.

This encounter is what began my journey to seek the Lord and to believe Him to be supernatural. The Book of Acts, as well as the life and ministry of Christ, shows us examples of the supernatural. God is saying that HIS same power lives in us, and we are being sent at an accelerated pace to be the manifestations of the Sons of God—now. The accounts of supernatural miracles that we read about in the scriptures are available to us—NOW.

Dances of the Supernatural occur when the power of God and the skill of dance are intertwined. Therefore, these dances are more of a paradigm than specific dance techniques, and they are for everybody. This book is designed to be a journey that seeks to provide revelation and strategies of how to function in the ministry of dance and operates in the supernatural through the dance. The journey begins by providing you with a foundation that is needed to serve in the overall ministry of dance. Then it leads to the dances of the supernatural that will teach you how to ascend in worship and descend in the supernatural power of God.

It is my prayer that, after reading this book, you will teach others and allow God to transform your dance. Allow Him to take you beyond the eight counts so that you can serve His people through love, which is the supernatural.

Part One

Before we jump into the river of the supernatural as it pertains to dance, it is important to have a solid foundation on why dance is a vital ministry in the Church (the Body of Christ). Everything that was made was made to worship God.

Dance is an expression in the earth
of the activity that occurs in Heaven.

I believe that we were created to move.
We were created to dance.

Take a baby for instance, if music is turned on they have a natural instinct to move. When we look at the trees or the ocean we see the world around us was made to respond to the presence and power of God through movement.

This serves as a foundation of the Supernatural because the Supernatural is very dependent upon our ability to move as God moves.

// KATRINA R. CARTER

Chapter One

CREATED TO DANCE

Exploring the Old Testament Scriptures reveals God's true intent for dance and establishes our identity as Servants of Dance. We were purposed for movement from the very beginning. We see in the Old Testament that everything that was made was made to praise Him. Scriptures in the Old Testament even reveals God's heart for the preparation of Christ's return.

We were created to dance. God had dancing in His Heart at the time of creation. *Genesis 1:2 says, "And the earth was without form and void and darkness was upon the face of the deep. And the Spirit of God moved upon the face of the waters".*

Here we see that, until God's first dance occurred, the Earth was empty and without shape. The word moved in this passage translates to the Hebrew word rachaph, which means to flutter, shake, hover *(Strong's H7363)*. The Earth had not been alive until this moment of choreography took place. Dance brings life to lifeless things and situations. God released his energy of life by dancing over the Earth, which was "without form and void." Here we see how God shifted a barren atmosphere to an atmosphere that is conducive to creativity and the newness of life. God desires for us to dance to continue to release His newness of life. He is a creative God. He reflects His creativity through His Ministers of Dance.

In the second chapter of Genesis we are told that once God breathed the breath of life into Adam, he became a living soul. This was essentially releasing Him to dance. The word living in this passage translates to the Hebrew word chay, meaning a person, place, or a thing is flowing, lively, active, renewed, and revived *(Strong's H2416)*. This word is an adjective that describes the state that Adam was in, and in turn, describes the state of being of dance ministry—that it does have a place in the Kingdom because it is a part of who we are. In dance, we have movements that flow and are lively. When we dance, we feel renewed and revived, as well as those who are watching. Dance was given to us at the time of creation because God had a plan for us to worship Him with dancing.

God has a natural response of movement. Dance, by definition, is movement to music, movement in a pattern of steps. It means to move merrily or rhythmically *(Dictionary.com)*. We were made in His image, so likewise, we were made to move. After this initial moment of dance, God continued to make things that moved. Everything that was made was made to give Him glory. He saw that it was good and danced! Animals have dance steps. The way the trees sway in the wind is a dance step. The lapping of the water in the oceans and seas is a dance step. *Psalm 98:8 says, "Let the floods clap their hands: let the hills be joyful together"*. Clapping in this verse is the word macha in Hebrew *(Strong's H4222)*. It means to strike, to clap the hands in exultation and joy. The sound the waters make is a praise unto God. They are clapping in celebration for who God is. Joyful in this verse comes from the Hebrew word ranan, or to overcome, to cry, to shout, to rejoice, to praise in exaltation *(Strong's H7442)*. God intends for us to respond to the glory of His hovering presence and for His glory! Psalm 98 is a prophetic song of victory and the Lord's salvation. Here we have this prophetic celebration dance of our coming King, and the outpouring of the Holy Spirit onto the Earth. Everything on the Earth was made to praise Him. Everything on the Earth was made to make His name great.

Dance is a common custom for those who believe. Dance is a part of our culture and who we are. In *Exodus 5:1*, the Lord says, *"And afterward Moses and Aaron went in, and told Pharaoh; Thus saith the Lord God of Israel, Let my people go that they may hold a feast unto me in the wilderness"*.

2

Aaron and Moses went to Pharaoh and told him that the Lord commanded that he let the Israelites go that they may have a feast in the wilderness. The first thing He commanded was that Pharaoh let His people go! The word go translates to the Hebrew term shalach, which means to send, to stretch out, to let go *(Strong's H7971)*. Then He stated that he wanted them to have a feast or a festival. The word feast translates to the Hebrew word chagag, or to move in a circle, to march in a sacred procession, and to observe a festival. God designed us to stretch and dance before Him. He designed us to go into the wilderness—into all the world to dance.

Dance is a response to the continual freedom that we have in Him. *Exodus 23:14 commands, "Three times thou shalt keep unto me a feast in the year".* The word feast in this scripture is also the same Hebrew word chagag *(H2287)*, meaning to dance, to move in a circle, to celebrate. God designed us to dance. He wants us to celebrate Him in movement. During this time in the Bible, God was giving the Israelites instructions on how He wanted them to live. He established laws on how He wanted them to observe the Shabbat. He established laws on how to be a good citizen. Then He established that He wanted them to dance before Him. As God was establishing their character and culture, he instilled in them the dance. God loves CELEBRATION!

Dancing Established Through the Feasts

There were three major feasts that God established in Exodus. These feasts are still observed annually with celebration and dancing. By establishing the Holy Feasts, God reveals to us why we dance, and some of the principles in which we are to live by. As servants of dance, we are to know why we're dancing or else we will be dancing amiss.

The Feast of Unleavened Bread (Passover) was celebrated in memorial of God, delivering the Israelites out of Egypt, marking the beginning of the Exodus. Exodus 12:13,14 says, *"The And the blood shall be to you for a token upon the houses where ye are and when*

I see the blood, I will pass over you, and the plague shall not be upon you to destroy you, when I smite the land of Egypt. And this day shall be unto you for a memorial; and ye shall keep it a feast to the LORD throughout your generations; ye shall keep it a feast by an ordinance forever."

During the Jewish Passover, the Israelites were to sacrifice a purified lamb and place its blood over the doorposts. This applied blood served as a sign so that the death angel would pass over the homes that were covered in the blood. After this event, the Israelites were encouraged to leave Egypt right away. Due to the swift departure, the Israelites had to make unleavened bread. This custom and time of deliverance is still celebrated today during the Passover on the Hebraic calendar, as well through the honoring of Triumphal Entry (Palm Sunday) and the Resurrection Day on the Gregorian calendar. These feasts are times of dancing that honor God's acts of redemption in the Old and New Testaments.

The term passover in Hebrew is the word pasach, meaning to leap, skip, spring over. God established a dance with a dance. Leaping is often times associated with joy. Even though God was executing judgment at the time, He was rejoicing over those who belonged to Him. He danced over the Israelites as an introduction to grace. He danced over the Israelites to rescue them from death and continues to dance over us today. This is also a type and shadow of what God would do for us in Christ. This dance speaks of how Jesus's redemptive blood would cover us and give us the freedom to dance. God also uses this event to establish one of the major feasts or dance celebrations in the Hebrew/Jewish culture.

The second major Feast or Dance in the Old Testament was the Feast of Weeks. This was the feast that occurred after the Passover feast. God ordained this feast through Moses. *Leviticus 23* says:

And ye shall count unto you from the morrow after the Sabbath, from the day that ye brought the sheaf of wave offering; seven Sabbaths shall be complete. Even unto the morrow after the seventh Sabbath shall ye number fifty days, and ye shall offer a new meat offering unto the Lord...forever in all your dwellings throughout your generations. And ye shall proclaim on the selfsame day, that it may be and holy convocation unto you: ye shall do no servile work therein: it shall be a statute and when ye reap the harvest of your Land, thou shalt not make clean riddance of the corners of thy field when thou reapest, neither shalt thou gather any gleaning of thy harvest thou shalt leave them unto the poor, and to the strange. I Am the Lord Your God.

This feast was established exactly 50 days after the Passover. We see this feast manifested in God's plan for redemption and reconciliation at Pentecost. *Acts 2:1* says, *"And when the day of Pentecost was fully come, they were all with one accord in one place."* The term Pentecost in this passage is the Greek word Pentekoste, which means the 50th day; it is the second of the three great Jewish Feasts, celebrated at Jerusalem yearly, the seventh week after the Passover, in grateful recognition of the completed harvest *(G4005)*. The Feast of Weeks is also a celebration of thanksgiving unto God.

The other significance of this feast is the heart of God that is revealed at the end of the passage. He gave specific instructions to leave the corners of the field untouched to provide for the poor *(Leviticus 23:22)*. This deals with the character of the dancer. We are to make sure that we give our gifts back to God and to make sure that we put others' needs above our own. We give our gifts back to Him by tithing and sowing into the cares and welfare of others. Keeping this concept of giving back in our hearts keep us in humble recognition that God is the source of our dance and He is to be given the First Fruit of our praise. We are to make sure that we understand that our dance is a service unto to God to be used for His glory.

The third feast that God designed just for rejoicing in dance was the Feast of Tabernacles. The Lord declares this as an ordinance for His people in scripture when He says, *"And the LORD spake unto Moses, saying, Speak unto the children of Israel, saying, The fifteenth day of this seventh month shall be the Feast of Tabernacles for seven days unto the LORD...And ye shall take you on the first day the boughs of goodly trees, branches of palm trees, and the boughs of thick trees, and willows of the brook; and ye shall rejoice before the LORD your God seven days. And ye shall keep it a feast unto the LORD seven days in the year. It shall be a statute forever in your generations: ye shall celebrate it in the seventh month" (Leviticus 23: 33-34, 40-41).*

The Feast of Tabernacles, also termed the Feast of Booths, was when the Israelites had to build small tents to remind them of the 40-year journey of their ancestors in the wilderness. During their 40 years in the wilderness, the Israelites had to build temporary structures to live in as they traveled to the Promised Land. The word rejoice in this passage is the Hebrew word samach, meaning to be glad to exult. God wanted the Israelites to come before Him rejoicing, and we are to continue to rejoice in Him. The word celebrate in this passage is the same previously stated Hebrew word chagag, meaning to hold a festival, to reel, to dance, to stagger. Its root word is chuwg, which means to make or draw a circle *(Strong's H2328 and H2287)*. God wanted the Israelites to praise Him with high praise and circle dances. The Feast of Tabernacles, for this reason, is also known as the most joyous feast.

Exploring the feast dances reveals to us the heart of God for dance and where the posture of our heart should be when we dance. Exploring other scriptures shows us the appropriateness of dancing before God and the reasons why we dance. In the article, "Finding Jesus in the Feast of Tabernacles," author David Brickner writes, "God gave Biblical festivals to teach the Jewish people about His character and to help us understand His plan for salvation" *(pg. 1)*. This same character is to be revealed in the dancer's lifestyle, as well in the choreographed or spontaneous dance. We were made in His Likeness and Image and should reflect Him in all that we do, including dance.

Dance as an Expression of Relationship

The first time the literal word dance was mentioned in scripture is in *Exodus 15:20*, which says, *"And Miriam the prophetess, the sister of Aaron took a timbrel in her hand: and all the women went out after her with timbrels and with dances"*. The word dance in this passage is the Hebrew word mechowlah, meaning to dance, to dance in a company. God parted the Red Sea, and the Israelites crossed over on dry land. Mariam danced in worship and praised God for delivering them from the attack of Pharaoh's army. This was a dance of victory. This same victory dance can be ministered as we reflect on the triumph of Christ at the cross.

Dancing is a sign of relationship. It was customary for the closest relative of the victor to greet the victor in celebration dances. Along with the story of Miriam, another time that the word dance is used is in Judges, when Jephthah returned home from battle with the Ammonites, and His daughter came to greet him with dances (*Judges 11:34*). Saul and David were greeted with dances upon David's return from slaying the Philistine (*I Sam 18:6*). Dancing in celebration of a returning King reflects the celebration dances of the Church and the Returning Christ. We should intensify our dancing in expectance of His return. *Matthew 24:44 says, "Therefore you must be ready, for the Son of Man is coming at an hour you do not expect"* (ESV). When our groom comes, we are to be prepared to greet Him with dances of joy, rejoicing, and jubilee.

This relationship with our King is where our worship comes from. Worship is a lifestyle that we are to seek with God. Our dance is birthed from this inner connection with God. Dance is to serve as an outward physical expression of the emotions, as well as the unctions that originate from the Holy Spirit, who lives in our spirit-man.

In a worship relationship with God, comes joy, rejoicing, peace, and intensified praise. David danced before God with all his might:

And David danced before the Lord with all his might; and David was girded with a linen Ephod. So David and all the house of Israel brought up the Ark of the Lord with shouting, and with the sound of the trumpet. And as the Ark of the Lord came into the city of David, Michal Saul's daughter looked through a window, and saw King David leaping and dancing before the Lord; and she despised Him in her heart. (I Samuel 6:14-16)

In context, the reason why David was dancing because of the return of the ark to Jerusalem, but the source of His dance was His worship relationship with God. The term danced in this passage comes from the Hebrew word karar, meaning to whirl *(Strong's H3769)*. Whirling, by definition, is to move or cause to move around and around. His love for God caused him to move around and around. Shouting is always a result of an emotion. Shouting in this passage is the Hebrew word teruwah, meaning to alarm, signal, shout a blast for war or joy, shout for joy with impulse, rejoice *(Strong's H8643)*.

David showed his worship relationship by shouting and rejoicing to God. His shout for joy was deepened by what the Lord did and shouted out of knowing that God was the source of his joy. God is to always be the source of our dance and praise, and we are to worship Him with all our might. The term leaping in this passage comes from the Hebrew word pazzaz, meaning to leap for joy, bound, spring up as a gazelle, be nimble, agile *(Strong's 6339)*. David's inner joy and love for God came springing up out of him and caused his body to respond by springing up with leaping.

Worship, by definition as a noun, is the feeling or expression of reverence and adoration for a deity. As a verb, worship means to show reverence and adoration for (a deity), honor with religious rites. Some of the synonyms are revere, exalt, glory *(Google Dictionary)*. A noun is a person, place, or a thing. Worship in this regard, then, is a person, place, and a thing. The person of God is our worship, the presence of God is our worship, and the feelings that we have towards Him is our worship. Worship is the essence of the dancer's heart. It goes beyond outside forces and comes from a place deep within us. An example of this is in *Job 1:20*, when the Bible says, *"Then Job arose, and rent His mantle, and shaved his head, and fell down upon the ground and worshipped".*

Job was responding to losing his livestock and his children. While external forces put him in a place of grief, His inward response to God was worship. The word worship in this passage is the Hebrew word shachah, meaning to depress, prostrate, bow down, crouch, fall down, humbly beseech, worship *(Strong's H7812)*. Job fell on his face in humility, honor, and trust of God's sovereignty. Even in his outward circumstance of devastation, His relationship with God allowed Job to remain submitted to Him. As minstrels of dance, we learn a lesson here. We learn that we are to remain humbled before God and that our worship must supersede any situation that we find ourselves in. We see through Job how to physically respond to God in humility.

This same prostrate position must be reflected in our character as well as in our dance. To lie prostrate is a sign of surrender and humility. This worship dance with God must continue even after the song is over and the garments are taken off. It is in this place of worship that we find the peace that Job had. I can imagine that in this position of worship and prostration, Job received the healing and refreshing that he needed to move forward after his loss.

Worshiping God in dance gives us a connection to God that causes us to triumph. We find this out in Joshua when the Lord spoke to Joshua and said:

And it shall come to pass that when they make a long blast with the ram's horn, and when ye hear the sound of the trumpet, all the people shall shout with a great shout, and the wall of the city fall down flat, and the people shall ascend up every man straight before him... And when it came to pass at the seventh time when the priests blew with the trumpet, Joshua said SHOUT: for the Lord hath given you the city. (Joshua 6:5, 16)

Joshua was given strategy by God that would cause him to triumph over the enemy. He was told that if they marched around Jericho seven times, on the seventh time, if they raised up a shout, the walls of Jericho would come down. It was in the shout that the triumph was declared and the wall came down. Shout in this passage comes from the Hebrew words ruwa and teruwa, meaning to raise a battle cry, to mar by breaking, triumph, rejoice *(Strong's H7321 & H8346)*. Shouting is both a sound and a movement to rejoice. It was in their rejoicing that the Lord moved on their behalf. As we shout and rejoice before God in dance, we will triumph over the enemy. Dancing, as seen in Joshua, is a strategy that God has blessed us with. Our praise then becomes our weapon to be used against the kingdom of darkness.

God reveals more of Himself to us through His dance with us. Spirit recognizes spirit. As we enter into His presence in worship and praise, there is a physical response to Him as our Father and Friend. *Psalm 96:4 says, "For the Lord is great and greatly to be praised: he is to be fear above all gods".*

Dancers are to have abandonment of self in the presence of God. Our focus is to give Him our all in all that we do along with our dancing. Our dance is to be free of distractions as we are to make our soul boast in the Lord so the humble shall hear and be glad (*Psalm 34:2*). Praising God with this kind of dance is contagious. We are to spread His name with our praise. As we spin, leap, kick, and wave our hands, He is exalted because this freedom is not something we could have established in and of ourselves. It comes from the worship relationship that we have with him.

We were made to praise and worship in dance before God. My favorite scripture is found in Malachi, and it declares, *"But unto you that fear my name shall the Sun of righteousness rise with healing in his wings. And you shall go out leaping like calves from the stall"* (*Malachi 4:2* ESV).

As we honor and serve God and others with our dancing, we will leap and be used by God to bring healing and joy to others. Dancing is a part of our character as established in the Feasts of the Lord. Dancing is a weapon that will cause us to triumph over our enemies. Dancing is a reflection of our relationship and nearness to God. Dancing will be how we greet our returning King as His bride. God has made us free to dance: "Let everything that has breath praise the Lord."

Supernatural Concepts Applied

1. *Dances of the Supernatural are reflected and cultivated through our relationship with God. What are ways that you can cultivate a deeper relationship with God to stimulate the supernatural in your life?*

2. *Why did God establish dance as a part of the Jewish culture, and what role does dance play in the present-day culture of the Kingdom of God?*

3. *We see in David that dance is a means of proclaiming our overcoming. What dance of overcoming do you need to proclaim? Write down what you need to overcome, and spend time each day dancing before God over those areas.*

Chapter Two

THE UNVEILED DANCE

Dance in the New Testament establishes dimension to our praise and worship. The New Testament gives us the details of how dance is to be represented on the Earth. The New Testament dancer is the manifestation of the Old Testament foundation of dance as a part of our identity. Studying dance as it relates to the new covenant reveals to the believer the dance that Jesus gave to us beyond the veil. Jesus established a new covenant for us at the cross. This NEW and better covenant establishes for us a NEW dance (*Hebrews 8:6*).

Matthew 27:51 says, "And behold the vail of the temple was rent twain from the top to the bottom; and the earth did quake, and the rocks rent." Now that we live the unveiled life, we also may minister the unveiled dance.

In order to serve as an unveiled dancer, we must understand the call and responsibility of the call. God has called us to be manifested sons through our dance. The New Testament dancer goes beyond the traditions of dance into a place of activating Heaven on Earth. *Romans 8:18, 19 says, "For I reckon that the sufferings of this present time are not worthy to be compared to the glory which shall be revealed in us. For the earnest expectation of the creature waiteth for the manifestation of the sons of God."*

The term wait here comes from the Greek word apekdechomai, which means to look to expect fully *(Strong's 553)*. Its unpacked meaning is to separate, depart, await *(Strong's G1551, G575)*. Its root denotes the origin or point from which action or motion proceeds, exceedingly, abundantly heavenly. Our worship originates from the Holy Spirit. As we die to self and yield to God, He is revealed through us. This yielding should not only occur when we're in the spotlight but also in our personal lives. Manifested Sons live in a way that glorifies God in our personal lives. Manifestation is translated to the Greek word apokalupsis, meaning to be revealed, revelation, disclosure, appearing, coming, lighten. This word comes from apocalupto, meaning to take off the cover, reveal, disclose *(Strong's G601 and G602)*. Manifested Sons live in a way that glorifies God in secret as well as in public. There are those who need to see God and the demonstrations of His power to believe. Having a servant's heart and understanding that the dance is not about us but about what God wants to do on the Earth for others is key. As we submit to God, He will cause us to be used of Him in mighty ways to the glory of God and the advancement of the Kingdom.

As New Testament dancers, we must seek God daily and ask ourselves what we are manifesting in our personal lives as well as through the dance. *II Corinthians 5:11 says, "Knowing therefore the terror of the Lord, we persuade men: but we are made manifest unto God; and I trust also are made manifest in your consciences".*

Manifest in this passage is the Greek word phaneroo, or to render apparent, declare, show oneself *(Strong's G5319)*. As we carry out God's character as New Testament believers, integrity is something that we must allow to be cultivated in us by studying scriptures. We must be the same person that is presented in garments as we are when the music stops and the spotlight is turned off. The anointing does not come with an on and off switch. The manifestation of the lifestyle of Kingdom dancing reveals to others who we are and sets us apart from this world.

The anointing is not only carried by how we dance but also by how we live. Jesus took off the cover so that we may dance freely and dance in the revelation of who He is and by His power. *Acts 17:28 says, "In Him we live, move, and have our being; as certain also of your own poets have said, For we are also His offspring."*

As God's children, we reflect Him on the Earth. Our dance and lifestyle is to be a reflection of the activity in Heaven and the nature of Christ. Our worship and praise says to the Earth, "Jesus is alive, and He is coming!"

An Audience of One

Kingdom advancement begins in the unveiled dancer as we separate ourselves from the world and yield to the Spirit of God living within us in our personal lives as well as when we minister in dance. Paul states in *I Corinthians 6:19*, *"What? Know ye not that your body is the temple of the Holy Ghost which is in you, which ye have of God and ye are not your own?"*.

We are not our own. The dance does not belong to us, but it is God's, and it is of God. With the indwelling and infilling of the Holy Spirit, we don't have to dance on our own strength; rather, as we yield to the presence of God living on the inside of us, the Holy Spirit dances through us. This is where we begin to see the difference between performance and ministry. Dance in and of itself is neutral; it's when we apply the intents and motives of the heart that makes it Kingdom worship or mere entertainment.

Dancing as an act of performance comes from the natural mind and seeks to please us and others. In ministry, the dance is birthed from God and seeks to please Him. The focus of performance dancing is the audience of many. In worship dance, there is an audience of one, and as we focus on our Father, he takes the dance and transforms it into manifestations of His power.

The first time the word dance is mentioned in the New Testament gives us an example of the difference between dancing to please God and dancing to please man—or the flesh.

Matthew 14:6-8 says: But when Herod's birthday was kept, the daughter of Herodias danced before them and pleased Herod. Where upon he promised her with an oath that he would give her whatsoever she would ask. And she being before instructed by her mother, said give me here John the Baptist's head in a charger.

Here we see the results of dancing in our own strength with the wrong motives to please someone other than God. The word danced in this passage translates to the Greek word orcheomai, meaning to dance in rank or to put in rapid motion *(Strong's G3738)*. The young girl, Solome, had the gift of dance, but her gift was perverted by the misguidance of her mother, Herodias. The fruit of her dance resulted in the death of John the Baptist. As ministers of sacred dance, we are to bear the good fruit of the Holy Spirit that leads to life.

John 10:10 says, "The thief cometh but for to steal, and to kill, and to destroy; I am come that they might have life, and that they may have it more abundantly".

As Spirit-filled believers, we are to dance under the empowering presence of God that releases life. When functioning in the supernatural, we have to remember that the enemy always seeks to twist the truth of God. There are two sources of the supernatural— the power of God and the false-power of Satan (witchcraft). When our motives and actions are not strictly of the Lord, then one is subject to the power of Satan. This is vital in understanding the supernatural because of the attempts of the enemy to counterfeit God's Word and Power.

Salome's dance was not protected, which allowed it to be twisted and used for evil instead of good. This reveals another truth that worshipers must be diligent in protecting their craft and the anointing that God places within us.

There is another message in this passage of scripture that we are to pay attention to. The reason why King Herod made the oath to give Salome anything she requested is because her dancing seduced him so that she obtained his favor. A worship dancer should never minister a dance that is void of the presence of God. As we dance before God, we are to make sure we are ministering with a pure heart of worship. Our worship is to come from our heart and to become conjoined with God's heart, thus causing Him to release His favor upon us. When this spirit-to-spirit connection is achieved, an environment conducive for the supernatural occurs.

Dancing under the new covenant is designed to reveal who God is. As we worship, God reveals Himself through the message of the dance. Everything that we release when we dance speaks a language, as dance is a universal language. In the book Let the Nations Rejoice, Dr. Pamela Hardy states, "Movement is a universal language that can transcend any language barrier" *(page 25)*.

Someone somewhere is waiting for us to communicate Heaven on Earth through our movement. For example, people are auditory learners, kinesthetic learners, or visuals learners. Dancing brings the message of God to the visual learners and builds their faith. Dancing by faith is the evidence of the presence and power of God. As we dance by faith, we encourage others in their faith. Dancing also brings the message of God to the kinesthetic learner in that physically dancing activates and imparts faith. *James 1:22 says, "But be ye doers of the word and not hearers only, deceiving your own-selves."*

The Lord always invites us to rejoice, praise, and worship Him not only in word but in our doing and living. In Luke 6:23, Jesus encouraged leaping when he said, "Rejoice ye in that day, and leap for joy: for behold, your reward is great in Heaven: for in like manner did their fathers unto the prophets." The word leap is translated to the Greek word skirtao, meaning to jump, leap for joy, or to skip *(Strong's 4640)*. Leaping communicates a message of joy and freedom. Leaping sends the message, *"If the Son shall make you free. Ye shall be free indeed" (John 8:36)*. The other working word in this passage is the verb rejoice. We are told several times throughout the New Testament to rejoice. The word rejoice can be translated to the Greek word chairo, meaning to be glad, well, or to salute. Jesus tells us to be glad. Rejoicing is not only a physical movement, but it is a mindset that every dancer must have.

Rejoicing speaks of an attitude of how we must come before God and His people. New Testament dancers must let this develop in them, which was also in Christ Jesus (*Philippians 2:5*). Even the attitude that we present can be used of God to build someone's faith. Our attitude towards our partners in ministry, towards those in authority over us, and towards ourselves also reflects our attitude towards God. Presenting ourselves in love and joy bears witness to the personality and character of Christ.

We are to present to Him our all with our whole being. Paul said in *Romans 12:1*, "*I beseech you therefore brethren by the mercies of God present your bodies a living sacrifice holy, acceptable to God, which is your reasonable service*".

To present comes from the Greek word paristemi, meaning to place beside or near, to place a person or a thing at one's disposal, to present a person for another to see and question, or to bring near *(Strong's G3936)*. As we dance, we should dance out of our nearness to God. We are to dance in excellence as yielded vessels committed to God. In the old covenant, the priests had to offer animals, but Christ came and established a new and better covenant as a final sacrifice. We, then, become a living sacrifice as we allow our dances to testify before Jesus as our covenant sacrifice. Therefore, out of celebration for what God has done for us through His son, Jesus Christ, we give ourselves to him. Dancing is the action that reflects the mindset of committing our all to Him. When we worship, leap, kick, twirl, run, etc. we are expressing to God that He can have it all.

Dancing as Representatives of Christ

Once we have taken on the mind of Christ concerning dance, we become in alignment with God's will to share the gospel through dance. One of the definitions of presenting, as mentioned before, is to present a person for another to see and question *(Strong's G3936)*. One of the purposes of dancing in the Church today is to present the person of Christ for others to learn of Him. In terms of discipleship, worship dance can be used as a means of evangelism and discipleship as we build teams within local fellowships, the community, and the nations.

Jesus commissions us in *Matthew 28:19, 20 when he says, "Go ye therefore, and teach all nations, baptizing them in the name of the Father, and of the Son, and of the Holy Ghost: Teaching them to observe all things whatsoever I have commanded you: and lo I am with you always".*

The word teach in this passage originates from the Greek word, matheteuo, meaning to make a disciple to instruct and to be a disciple to follow His precepts and instructions (Strong's G3101). He told us to both be a disciple and make disciples. To advance the Kingdom, we must reproduce after Christ. The command was to go! Jesus did not specify by what means we are supposed to make disciples; rather, in all God's creativity, He gave us various gifts and graces to use to make disciples. Dancing is one of those avenues that can be used to be a disciple and make disciples. Dancing is a powerful delivery system because it is unique and can be adapted to any group as we seek the Lord for wisdom. For example, by learning dances that are native to a specific culture or country allows servants of the dance to reach that group with efficacy.

We must seek the Lord to show us the bigger picture of dance ministry and to show us how not to become stagnant in Sunday praise, worship, and choreographed pieces. We must be willing to go into all nations and share the gospel of truth through dance. Paul said in *I Corinthians 9:19-23*:

For though I be free from all men, yet I have made myself servant unto all, that I might gain the more. And unto the Jews that I might gain the Jews; to them that are under the law, that I might gain them that are under the law; To them that are without law, as without law (being not without law to God, but under the law to Christ,) that I might gain them that are, without law. To the weak became I as weak: I am made all things to all men, that I might by all means save some."

Paul saw the bigger picture—that we must have the tenacity to reach people by all means. The Lord wants to see all souls saved and reconciled back to Him. Paul understood that he did not have to compromise His faith at all. He did not seek to please man; rather, he became like a chameleon as a strategy to spread the good news. As dancers, we have the God-given ability to do the same. This is why we must continue to not only sharpen the craft of dance itself but sharpen our perception in the Spirit. Evangelizing the gospel as led by the Spirit of the Lord is one of the fruits of the New Testament dancer.

Jesus is our Prochorus! In *Acts 6:5*, when the seven deacons were appointed, it says, *"And the saying pleased the whole multitude: and they chose Stephen, a man full of faith and of the Holy Ghost, and Phillip, and Prochorus, and Nicanor, and Timon, and Parmenas, and Nicolas a proselyte of Antioch…".*

The name prochorus in this passage can be translated to the Greek word prochoros, which means before the dance. This word has an unpacked revelation. Pro means in front of, prior, above, superior, before, and choros means round dance (choir). This passage speaks to all dance ministers, and it leaves a specific message to those who are in leadership. It says to the dance ministers that we are to only dance what he tells us to, and when He tells us to. We are not to add to, nor take away from, His dance. To the dance leader: We are to look to Christ to lead us. We are to lead our teams only as He leads us.

In regards to both the individual dancer and the dance leader, we must make sure we submit to God at all times. *Romans 8:14, 16 says, "For as many as are led by the Spirit of God, they are the sons of God. The Spirit itself beareth witness with our spirit, that we are the children of God".* Ensuring that we are being led by God when leading our teams and our individual dance identifies us in the natural as Spirit-filled dancers. This is what sets worship dance apart from ordinary dance. It also identifies us in the spirit as a chosen people who belong to God. The sacred dance shares the personality and character of Christ. Dancing has always been a part of our identity. Jesus came so that we could be able to dance before our Father freely, with Christ, Himself, being our dance leader.

Dance originated in the Spirit of God at the beginning and never lost its place nor its power in the New Testament Church. The New Testament dancer takes the Old Testament foundation and goes into dimensions that lead to kingdom advancement. To do this, the dancer must be willing to minister from a place of revelation or the revealed truth of God's Word. We must learn to dance our revelation.

There must be a crossover from being just a dancer to being a servant of the Lord in dance. *I Peter 4:10,11 says, "As every man has received the gift, even so speak as the oracles of God; if any man minister let him do it as of the ability which God giveth: that God in all things may be glorified through Jesus Christ, to whom be praise and dominion forever and ever."*

The verb minister in this passage translates from the Greek word diakoneo, meaning to wait upon as a host, friend, or teacher; to serve; to use the office of a deacon. We are to use the gift of dance to serve others. Specifically, we are to be rooted in love, share the gift of dance by teaching others the ministry of dance, and care for the needs of others around us. The word praise in this passage comes from the Greek word doxa, meaning to honor, praise, worship a deity *(Strong's G1391)*. Its root word is dieknuo, meaning to show, shew. Dancing allows us to show our praise to God on the Earth. Dancing is the showing of the same servanthood Christ exemplified during His time here on the Earth.

Our worship is an expression of the grace that was given to us at the cross. *Ephesians 2:8 says, "For by grace are ye saved through faith; and that not of yourselves: it is the gift of God"*. Grace is a gift in itself, and dancing is one of the manifestations of God's grace. Grace is defined as "the love and mercy given to us by God because God desires for us to have it, not because of anything we have done to earn it" *(Wikipedia.com)*. Dancing is a gift graced to us by God. It is not earned; rather it is bestowed upon us by God. Therefore we are to dance with humility. This humility begins with our worship as a lifestyle.

Humility is a principle found in *John 4:23, 24*, when Jesus says, *"But the hour cometh, and now is, when the true worshippers shall worship the Father in spirit and in truth: for the Father seeketh such to worship Him. God is a Spirit: and they that worship Him must worship Him in spirit and in truth".*

Worship, in this passage, originates from the Greek word proskuneo. It means to kiss the hand towards one in token of reverence, fall upon the knees and touch the ground, kneel or lie in prostration to do homage whether to express respect or supplication *(Strong's G4352)*. It is where our English word prostrate also comes from. Not only are we to physically prostrate ourselves, but we are to prostrate our spirit and hearts towards God. God wants our life as well as our dance. When we worship, we are saying to God that we recognize we belong to Him, and everything that we do belongs to Him. Every dance should begin, end, and be consumed by worship as a reflection of God's grace. Worship activates the intimacy that we have with God under the new covenant.

Worship reflects the activity in Heaven. *Revelation 4:10-11 says, "The four and twenty elders fall down before him that sat on the throne, saying, 'Thou art worthy, O Lord, to receive glory and honour and power: for thou hast created all things, and for thy pleasure they are and were created.'*

The words fall down in this passage translate to the Greek word pipto, and means to fall, go from an erect position to a prostrate position, prostrate oneself, lose authority *(Strong's G4098)*. As we fall down in worship to our Lord, we are saying that we recognize he is in authority over us as Lord of our lives. We are joining in with Heaven to declare that God is the one true God and ruler of all things.

We did not earn the gift of dance, God in His sovereignty gave it to us. Dance is a reflection of the restoration that we were given through Christ. We see this type of dancing in *Luke 15:20, 25: "And he arose, and came to his father. But when he was yet a great way off, his father saw him, and had compassion, and ran, and fell on his neck, and kissed him... Now his elder son was in the field: and as he came and drew nigh to the house, he heard musick and dancing".*

The father embraced his son physically and with dancing. Dancing, in this passage, is the Greek word choros, or to dance in a ring, or a round dance. The people danced to celebrate the returning of the lost son. Here we see that dance was already established as part of the identity of the people, and because of that principle, the prodigal son was welcomed by his closest relative (his father) with a feast and dancing. As unveiled dancers, we must extend the grace message of restoration to those that we serve. The son felt like what he did by leaving made him unworthy of his father's love because of his rebellion, but his father received him with open arms—how our Father receives us. This is an example of God's grace. Unveiled dancers must seek to embrace God's grace and extend His grace through dance. The new covenant worshiper is to minister this message that our Father loves us and is embracing us with His grace.

Sent to Manifest

The new covenant dancer is sent to function as one who releases the Holy Spirit as (s)he ministers. Outward signs of the inward working of the Holy Spirit are manifested through dancing. We see an example of this in *Acts 3:6-9*, and it says:

"Then Peter said, Silver and Gold have I none; but such as I have, give I thee: In the name of Jesus Christ of Nazareth rise up and walk. And he took him by the right hand, and lift him up: and immediately his feet and ankles bones received strength, and he leaping up stood, and walked, and entered with them into the temple, walking, and leaping and praising God. And all the people saw him walking and praising God."

Peter did not have what the man wanted but offered what he could give, which was in turn what the man needed. As ministers, we are to offer ourselves and our praise back to God. As we yield to Him, He will—by the power of His Spirit—cause Himself to be manifested on the Earth. Peter lifted the man. One of the fruits of dance as a ministry of love is that we are to leave God's people feeling lifted. At that moment, the transference of healing and faith occurs. As we minister by faith, God will do the healing, delivering, restoring, and more.

In verse 8 of this passage, the word leaping is mentioned twice and has two translations in Greek. The first translation comes in Acts 3:8a, from the Greek word exallomai, meaning to spring forth *(Strong's G1814)*. Its root word is the word ex, which denotes the point or origin from which motions proceeds; out of a place, time, or cause *(Strong's G1537)*. The lame man sprung out of his previous physical state into a state of leaping and praising God (dancing). The second translation for the word, as ascribed in Acts 3:8b, is the Greek word hallomai, meaning to jump, gush, leap, or spring up *(Strong's 242)*. The result of the lame man's physical healing was an inner joy that transformed into leaping. Through this story, we still see that dancing is a natural reaction to an inward feeling from God that is birthed from a connection to God as the source of our rejoicing.

As unveiled ministers of dance, our heart of worship towards God causes us to leap before Him, bringing about transformation in the lives of others. Through our leaping and dancing before the Lord, He will also cause us as well as those He sends us to serve to go from one state to another. In this passage, dancing (specifically leaping) is a demonstration of God's power. The man was healed, and as a sign of his healing, he leaped and praised God—something that He could not do before. God will take us to new dimensions in our praise as we demonstrate His power on the Earth.

God wants continual rejoicing from His people as we wait for our King to return. *Revelation 19:7 says, "Let us be glad and rejoice, and give honour to him: for the marriage of the Lamb is come, and his wife hath made herself ready"*. Rejoice, in this passage, is translated from the Greek word agalliao and means to jump for joy, exult, be exceedingly glad, jump with exceeding joy *(Strong's G21)*. As the brides of Christ, we are the closest female relative to Him. When he returns, we are to welcome Him with rejoicing, revealing that we can never stop dancing.

The New Testament worshiper carries out and lives the Old Testament foundation and principles. In this regard, we see the reflection of Christ and the life application of the dance working through the New Testament Church. The New Testament Church understood their identity, which included, and still includes, the unveiled dance.

Supernatural Concepts Applied

1. *Write a mission statement of how you plan to carry out your identity as a new covenant worshiper.*

2. *What is one thing that you can implement in your choreography and/or praise and worship services to ensure that you are uplifting others while you are ministering in dance?*

3. *Dance is a sign of the restoration in the relationship between God and man. What message(s) do you feel you are sent to share with others?*

Chapter Three

DANCING THROUGH THE TABERNACLES:
Coming of Ages

God With Us

God desired to be with us and to establish a relationship with us. *Genesis 1:26 says, "Let us make man in our image, after our likeness: and let them have dominion…".*

Being created in God's image gave mankind a unique relationship with him. This is what separates mankind from the rest of creation. Being created in the image of God established the father-son relationship man and God. For example, when a parent has a child, that child tends to look like and carry the traits of their parent. By creating man, God revealed His will to have love, fellowship, and intimacy with His people.

In *Genesis 2:8*, the Lord established a dwelling place for man. It says, *"And the Lord God planted a garden eastward in Eden; and there he put the man whom he had formed"*. Once God created man, He gave him a physical place to live with Him. Eden has the same name in Hebrew and means pleasure, delight. It was the first habitat of man after the creation *(Strong's H5727)*.

Eden was not only a physical dwelling place for man, but it also represented a state of being between man and God. This is why researchers can't physically locate the garden. In the article, "The Lost Rivers of the Garden of Eden," the author states, "Nobody has been able to look at modern maps of the regions mentioned in Genesis and figure out exactly where the Garden of Eden was,

at least by the present topography of the lands of the Middle East"
(The Bible Genesis and Geology/kjvbible.org).

God delighted in His creation, and Adam had luxuries—blessings
from his direct connection with God. Before the fall of man, God
had direct communication and delight with man. After the fall of
man, God established things that would lead us back to Eden or
divine fellowship with Him. *Psalm 43:3 says, "O send out your light
and your truth: let them lead me; let them bring me to your holy hill,
and to your tabernacles".* Once man fell, they lost the physical access
to Eden and the spiritual state of being of Eden that was previously
held with God. God never lost His desire to dwell with, and be one
with, man.

In his sermon, "Eden-God's Presence," Dr. Myles Monroe stated:

Eden is a spot or moment where the Presence of God is an open
door to Heaven. God took a piece of Heaven and touched earth.
Man was placed in the presence of God, in complete communion
with God. *(International Worship Institute Dallas, TX 2002)*

Eden was not a specific place but represented God's presence filling
the Earth. *Isaiah 6:3 says, "And they were calling to one another and
said Holy, Holy, Holy is the Lord of hosts: the whole Earth is filled with
His glory".* God desires that His presence overtakes the Earth. He
desires Heaven on Earth. He desires these moments in time where
His presence touches us. At the time of creation, Eden was a type
of tabernacle that would later be manifested in the Tabernacle of
Moses, the Tabernacle of David, completed through Jesus Christ as
our finished, living tabernacle, and we, God's people, as tabernacles
with the indwelling of the Holy Spirit.

The tabernacles were symbolic of a progression to restoration
between God and man. We see this progression in the differences
of the Tabernacle of Moses and the Tabernacle of David. After the
fall, God put things, such as the tabernacles, in place so that would
lead us to Christ and back to Eden with Him.

God Established Us

Exodus 25:8, 9 says, "And let them make me a sanctuary; that I may dwell amongst them". The word sanctuary in this passage comes from the Hebrew word miqdash. It is a holy place, a sacred place, a sacred temple *(Strong's H4720)*. Its origin comes from the Hebrew word qadash, meaning to be set apart, be consecrated, hallowed, treated as sacred. The Tabernacle of Moses was set apart from everything else. It was in the center of the camp in the wilderness. This denotes the intent of God's heart and the purpose of the tabernacle mentioned in the latter part of *Exodus 25:8*. God's desire was, and still is, to dwell among us. The word dwell in this passage comes from the Hebrew word shakan and means to settle down, reside, establish. God was establishing His presence and relationship with man. This is how Jesus would come to dwell among us in person during his time on the Earth. *John 1:14 says, "And the Word was made flesh, and dwelt among us, and we beheld his glory, the glory as of the only begotten of the Father full of grace and truth".*

The Greek word for dwell in this passage is skenoo, to fix one's tabernacle, live in a tabernacle *(Strong's G4737)*. Its root meaning comes from the word skenos, meaning tabernacle or tent, the human body where the soul dwells *(Strong's G4636)*. Jesus came as our living tabernacle.

The Tabernacle of Moses further points to Christ in its construction, and God's redemptive plan. *Exodus 25:9 says, "According to all that I shew thee, after the pattern of the tabernacle, and the pattern of all the instruments thereof, even so shall ye make it".*

This passage carries the first mention of the tabernacle; it translates to the Hebrew word mishkan and means dwelling place or tent, habitation, or a residence *(Strong's 4908)*. The tabernacle was to be a place where God lived with His people. The tabernacle, being built within a temporary tent, reveals that it was symbolic of a progression to a larger goal. The root meaning of tabernacle comes from the word shakan, and means to settle down, establish, fix

(Strong's H7931). The Tabernacle of Moses was symbolic of how God sought to repair mankind from its sinful nature. The Tabernacle of Moses established the foundation, which had been previously laid between man and God at the time of creation. It also established the foundation of the Mosaic Law as was given to Moses at Mt. Sinai.

The Tabernacle of David also was a temporary fixture that pointed to something greater. I*saiah 16:5 says, "And in mercy shall the throne: be established: and he shall sit upon it in truth in the Tabernacle of David, judging, and seeking judgment, and hasting righteousness".* The word tabernacle in this passage originates from the Hebrew word ohel and means a nomadic tent, clearly conspicuous from a distance, covering *(Strong's H168).* Its root meaning is the Hebrew word ahal, to be clear, shine *(Strong's H166).* While both tabernacles were the center of attention in the camp, the Tabernacle of David pointed to a new order of worship. The word ahal is similar to the Hebrew word for praise, halal, which also means to be clear, shine, boast, clamorously foolish *(Strong's H194).* The Tabernacle of David produced a birthing of worship as we see it today. With God as our covering, we are to make Him shine in our tabernacles or tents of meeting, also known as the local fellowship.

The Lord told Moses to make the tabernacle after a specific pattern. In his book, The Tabernacle of Moses, author Kevin J. Conner states, "Everything was to be made according to God's pattern. God can only bless and seal with glory that which is done according to the standard of His Word" *(p.10).* How Moses constructed the tabernacle was reflective of how he adhered to God's Word. David had to follow God's specific instructions for transporting the Ark of the Covenant. This is also a relevant application for today. We must study and adhere to God's precepts as taught in the scriptures.

God for Us - The Messianic Age

The progressive patterns in the structure of both tabernacles points to the dispensations or ages of how God deals with man. Paul states in *Ephesians 1:10, "That in the dispensation of the fullness of times he might gather together in one all things in Christ, both which are in Heaven, and which are on the earth: even in Him".* The Greek translation of the word dispensation is the word oikonomia and is the management of a household or the management of affairs, stewardship. *(Strong's G3622).* The Tabernacles of Moses and David differed in how they were managed and in how the affairs transpired within them. Both play an important role in the development and history of the Church body and church services as we know them today.

The Tabernacle of Moses contained three parts: the outer court, the holy place, and the most holy place. Each section contained specific furniture and activities that would be manifested by Christ. Each section of the Tabernacle of Moses, along with the activities and furniture, was symbolic of a coming dispensation.

Scripturally, the first section of the tabernacle that was built was the Ark of the Covenant, which dwelled in the Most Holy Place. God's ultimate goal of communing with man is revealed in the order by which Moses was to build the tabernacle. *Exodus 25:10 says, "And they shall make an ark of shittim wood...".* The first piece of the tabernacle that God told Moses to build was the Ark of the Covenant. It was to go in the Most Holy Place. Everything begins and ends with God. *John 1:1, 2 says, "In the beginning was the Word and the Word was with God and the Word was God. The same was in the beginning with God".*

The Most Holy Place reveals the dispensation of the Messianic Kingdom. This is God's ultimate goal for us to be in his presence, one on one and face to face. In the article, "Jesus in the Tabernacle Bible Study," author I. Gordon states, "This area represents the coming of the Kingdom age where God shall dwell among His people once again in visible form. In terms of the aspect of a Believers salvation it represents our 'glorification' where we are with Christ and are like Christ" *(jesusplusnothing.com)*.

The Ark of the Covenant was also called the Ark of the Testimony because of what was contained within it. Within the ark was the jar of manna:

And Moses said unto Aaron, take a pot, and put an omer full of manna therein, and lay it up before the Lord, to be kept for your generations. As the Lord commanded Moses, so Aaron laid it before the Testimony to be kept. (Exodus 16:33)

The jar of manna was a testament of how the Lord provided for the Israelites in the wilderness. It was the son of God as the bread of life. The word testimony in this passage comes from the Hebrew word eduwth and means a precept of God, witness, or law *(Strong's H5715)*. This word breaks down into two unpacked root meanings. The first is the Hebrew word ed, meaning to witness against, legislator, commander *(Strong's 5707)*. The ark carried with it God's judgment of sin. The second part of the root meaning is uwd and means to restore, relieve, testify, do over again *(Strong's H5749)*. God was putting in place the opportunity for man to start over. Jesus said in *John 6:51, "I am the living Bread which came down from Heaven: if any man eat of this bread, he shall live forever, and the bread that I will give is my flesh which I will give for the life of the world"*.

Christ offers us something that was not previously available to us— everlasting life. Christ is our manna.

Along with the jar of manna, the Ark of the Covenant contained within it Aaron's rod. *Numbers 17:8, 10 says: And it came to pass that on the morrow Moses went into the tabernacle of Witness: and behold, the rod of Aaron for the house of Levi was budded, and brought forth buds, and bloomed blossoms, and yielded almonds... And the Lord said unto Moses, Bring Aarons rod again before the Testimony to be kept for a token against the rebels.*

The word witness has the same translation and meaning as the word testimony. Here we see that another precept (law) was planted within the ark. The word rod is translated to the Hebrew word matteh and is a staff, branch, vine, or company led by a chief *(Strong's H4294)*. The rod foreshadowed the coming Messiah, His resurrection, and our salvation. Christ is the vine, and we are the branches. The rod budded and blossomed out of something dead. *John 15:2 says, "Every branch in me that beareth not fruit he taketh away: and every branch that beareth fruit he purgeth it, that it may bring forth more fruit".*

The rod also reveals the fruit of the Holy Spirit. The rod bearing fruit within the ark is how the indwelling Holy Spirit bears fruit in us. The Ark of the Covenant contained the tablets with the written Ten Commandments on them. *Deuteronomy 10:5 says, "And I turned myself and came down from the mount, and put the tables in the ark which I had made; and there they be, as the Lord commanded me".*

Kevin Conner says, "Here we see a type of the Father-God, the Lawgiver...the Law is symbolic of all authority and power which is in the hands of the Father" *(The Tabernacle of Moses p.27)*. Within the Ark of the Covenant were elements that represented the triune God Himself. At the time of its construction, only the High Priest had access to the Most Holy Place. During the Messianic Age or dispensation, all will have access to the presence of God and will be in fellowship just like at the Garden of Eden.

God Among Us - The Dispensation of Grace

The holy place contained specific furniture and activity that reveal the dispensation grace, and God's plan for salvation. The golden lampstand provided light in the holy place. *Leviticus 24:2 says, "Command the Children of Israel that they bring unto thee pure oil olive beaten for the light to cause the lamps to burn continually".*

Light in this passage is the Hebrew word ma'owr *(Strong's H3974)*. It is luminary. Its meaning is found in its root word owr and means to enlighten, shine, give light; glorious *(Strong's H215)*. It represents the light of Christ. Jesus says in *John 8:12*, *"I am the light of the world. He that followeth me will never walk in darkness, but will have the light of life"*.

The word light in this passage translates from the Greek word phos and means to emit light, a lamp, heavenly light, brilliant, that which is exposed to all. The lamp in the Tabernacle of Moses was also symbolic of the light God provided for the children of Israel as they traveled through the wilderness. When the cloud moved, the Israelites knew that it was time to move, and when the cloud stopped, the Israelites knew it was time to settle. The Tabernacle of David allowed the Most Holy Place to be exposed to the view of all, just as Christ was exposed to the view of all when He hung on the cross. Christ was establishing His light in us as He was/is light, and the source of light in darkness. In both tabernacles, we have the message that we are to be followers of the light. When the light moves, we are to move with Him.

The Altar of Incense was also located in the holy place. The Altar of Incense was to be burnt constantly in the Tabernacle of Moses. *Exodus 30:35 says, "And thou shalt make it a perfume, of it very small, and put of it before the testimony in the tabernacle of the congregation, where I will meet with thee: it shall be unto you most holy"*.

The word perfume in this passage is the Hebrew word q'toreth and means fumigation, sweet incense. Its meaning in root comes from the Hebrew word qatar and means to fumigate in a close place, drive out occupants, smoke, or to turn into fragrance by fire. The incense, in the natural, drove out the smells of the burnt offerings that were sacrificed on the Brazen Altar. In the spirit, the smoke and smell drove out the presence of anything that was not like God. Today, our prayer, praise, worship, and intercession drive out the presence of any flesh. This driving out not only takes place in the atmosphere around us, but also in us. *I Corinthians 1:29, 30 says, "That no flesh should glory in his presence. But of him are ye in Christ*

Jesus, who of God is made unto us righteousness and sanctification and redemption...".

The incense was made of a special recipe that could not be reproduced. Righteousness, sanctification, and redemption are the special ingredients of our incense given to us by Christ, which cannot be reproduced. This recipe is how we are able to draw near to Christ.

The Golden Altar of Incense was located closest to the Ark of the Covenant and at the heart of the Tabernacle of Moses. "From all this we see that the ministry of intercession, prayer, and praise are at the very heart of God, These are the nearest things closest to God" *(Conner, The Tabernacle of Moses, p.49)*. The Altar of Incense was not a part of the Tabernacle of David. Instead, David installed ministries that were carried out by the people. These ministries shape the way we worship today. Included is a chart that reveals the elements of worship that were established through the Tabernacle of David as we experience them today.

The Evolution of Today's Worship

Expression of Worship in the Tabernacle of David	Scripture Reference	What We See in Worship Today
The Ministry of Singing and Singers	I Chronicles 15:16-27; 25:1-7	Praise and Worship Teams, Choirs, and Prophetic Singers
The Ministry of Musicians with Instruments	I Chronicles 23:5 and 25:1-7	Bands, Music Ministry, Organist, Keyboardist, Violinist, Percussionist, etc. (All Instruments)
The Ministry of Levites Before the Ark	I Chronicles 16:4, 6, 37	The Minister of Music and Arts, The Five Fold Ministry
The Ministry of Recording	I Chronicles 16:4, 8, 41 and Psalm 116:7	Media Ministries, Photography, Prophetic Painting, Scribes who Document Services, Journaling, All Believers

Expression of Worship in the Tabernacle of David	Scripture Reference	What We See in Worship Today
The Ministry of Thanking the Lord	I Chronicles 16:4, 8, 41; Psalm 116:17 II Chronicles 29:30, 31	Intercessors, Individual & Corporate Prayer, All Believers
The Ministry of Praise	I Chronicles 6:4, 36	Ministers of Dance and Movement, Ministers of Song & Music, Artistic Ministries
The Ministry of Psalms	I Chronicles 16:9 and Psalm 98:5-6	Minister of Music, All Believers
The Ministry of Rejoicing and Joy	I Chronicles 16:10, 16:25-31	Ministers of Dance and Movement, Corporate Worship
The Ministry of Clapping Hands	Psalm 47:1 and Psalm 98:8	Ministers of Dance and Movement
The Ministry of Shouting	I Chronicles 15:28 and Psalm 47:1	Corporate Worship
The Ministry of Dancing	I Chronicles 15:29; II Samuel 6:14; Psalm 149:3 and Psalm 150:4	Ministers of Dance and Movement
The Ministry of Lifting Up the Hands	Psalm 141:2 and Psalm 134:2	All Believers
The Ministry of Worship	I Chronicles 15:29; Psalm 29:1-2; Psalm 95:6	All Believers
The Ministry of Seeking the Lord	I Chronicles 16:10-11; II Chronicles 7:14	All Believers Studying Scriptures, Prayer, Praise, Worship
The Ministry of Spiritual Sacrifices	Psalm 27:6 (joy) Psalm 116:17 (thanksgiving)	All Believers
The Ministry of Saying Amen	I Chronicles 16:36	All Believers

The ministries implemented in the Tabernacle of David pointed to the dispensation of grace. Under grace, we have access to worship the Father and dwell with Him in His presence. The Age of the Church is where we, the people, carry out the principals and truths found in both tabernacles.

Along with the Golden Lampstand and the Altar of Incense was the Table of the Bread of the Presence. On the table were twelve loaves of bread that represented the twelve tribes of Israel.

Exodus 25:30 says, "And thou shalt set upon the table shewbread before me alway".

This ordinance is echoed by Jesus in *I Corinthians 11:24, "And when he had given thanks, he break it and said, 'Take, eat: this is my body which is broken for you; do this in remembrance of me'".*

The priests had to eat the bread and replenish the bread on every Sabbath day. One of the names of God is the Bread of Life. The table of showbread symbolized God's covenant provision as provider for the twelve tribes of Israel. Christ is the manifestation of the bread of life for us. He is also the giver of life to all who follow Him.

The table of showbread was of the new covenant that would be fulfilled by Christ. *Jeremiah 31:31-34 says:*

Behold, the days to come, saith the Lord, that I will make a new covenant with the house of Israel and with the House of Judah: Not according to the covenant that I made with their fathers in the day that I took them by the hand, to bring them out of the land of Egypt; which my covenant they break, although I was a husband to them saith the Lord: But this shall be the covenant that I will make with the house of Israel; After those days, saith the Lord I shall put my law in their inward parts, and write it in their hearts; and will be their God, and they shall be my people. And they shall teach no more every man his neighbor, and every man his brother saying, Know the Lord: for they shall all know me from the least of them to the greatest of them, saith the Lord; for I will forgive their iniquity, and remember their sin no more.

God made a promise that He would send to us a savior that would live in us and grant us a personal relationship with Him. The word know in this passage is the Hebrew word yada and means to know, be acquainted with, perceive, distinguish, reveal oneself *(Strong's 3045)*. Yada is the root word for one of the Hebrew words for praise, yadah. Yadah means to hold out the hand, to revere or worship with extended hands. Through the Tabernacle of David, the ministry of lifting up the hands and thanking the Lord was instituted.

These acts are still done today in services, in our conversation, and in our private time with God. We express that we are acquainted with His presence by lifting our hands and by thanking Him for who He is to us. When a child's father comes home, the child runs to their father with extended and lifted hands. When we lift our hands, we are like that small child running to our Father. The lifting of the hands shows that we have a distinguished relationship with our Creator. *Romans 8:15 says, "For ye have not received the spirit of bondage again to fear; but ye have received the Spirit of adoption whereby we cry we cry Abba, Father".*

The eating of the bread was in line with the cultural identity of the people of Israel, as the eating of bread or the sharing of a meal was done to seal a covenant. It pointed to what Jesus said at the Lord's Supper: *"For as often as ye eat this Bread and drink this cup, ye do show the Lord's death till He come" (I Corinthians 11:26).* The bread represented His body and the body of Christ. The cup represented Christ's blood. To eat the bread and drink the cup showed agreement to the covenant established by Christ. In the Tabernacle of David, this agreement was carried out through the ministry of saying, "Amen." *I Chronicles 16:36 says, "Blessed be the Lord God of Israel for ever and ever. And all the people said, Amen, and praised the Lord".* The phrase amen in this passage comes from the same Hebrew word amen and means sure, faithfulness, so be it *(Strong's 543)*. Its meaning in root is the Hebrew word aman and means to build up or support, render, trust, or to believe, go to the right hand, assurance *(Strong's 539)*.

Saying "amen" confirms our assurance of salvation and our trust in Christ and confirms that we believe. Our "amen" is affirmed through the act of communion. This is also why communion is taken at weddings and even in the privacy of the home. Communion reminds us of Christ as our Savior and the covenant relationship established with Him at the time of salvation. To eat a meal together is a form of fellowship. Communion signifies our fellowship with Christ and the divine communion that is restored to us with God through Christ. And we all still say, "Amen!"

Our amen comes from our belief in the death, burial, resurrection, and the ascension of Christ. It is when we accept Christ as Lord and Savior that we are no longer separated from God. In the Tabernacle of Moses, the veil was the partition that separated the holy place from the most holy place. *Exodus 26:33 says, "And thou shalt hang up the vail under the taches, that though mayest bring in thither within the vail the Ark of the Testimony and the vail shall divide unto you between the holy place and the most holy".*

A veil is a curtain. Its root meaning comes from the Hebrew word perek meaning cruelty, severity, harshness, or oppression *(Strong's 6531)*. The veil represents the judgment of sin and the penalty of sin—separation from God. In this regard, the veil represents the law. *Ephesians 2:14 says, "For he is our peace who hath us both one and has broken down the middle wall of partition between us".*

A partition is something that separates or divides into portions or shares *(Dictionary.com)*. When Adam sinned in the Garden of Eden, man was separated from God and His presence, thus causing a wall to be put up between man and God. The veil speaks to the Adamic nature of man in that the sins of man that once separated us from God. Only the High Priest had access to go behind the veil, and he could only go on the day of atonement (Yom Kippur). The veil represented the need for atonement and restored access. With the High Priest being the only one who could go beyond the veil, the veil also foreshadowed our coming High Priest.

The renting of the veil signifies the transference from being under the old covenant of the Law to the new covenant of grace. Kevin J. Conner wrote, "In making the Mosaic Covenant old, it marked the ushering in of the new covenant to which all of the external form of the Mosaic Covenant pointed. It ushered in all of the realities which had been hidden in the external form" *(p.69). Mark 15:38 says, "And the vail was rent in twain from top to bottom".*

The word rent in this passage originates from the Greek word schizo and means to cleave asunder, divide by rending, split into factions *(Strong's G4977)*. The renting of the veil from top to bottom denotes that this was the moment that the Presence of Heaven touched the Earth. It was a sign that the direct access to God's presence had been restored back to its original state just as it was in the Garden of Eden. The moment that Jesus died for us, the veil that separated us from God's presence was done away with because Jesus became the blood sacrifice for our sins. That day marked the final day of atonement.

The outer court speaks to the dispensation of the Mosaic Law. The outer contained the Brazen Altar, the Bronze Laver. The Brazen Altar was an altar of sacrifice and was used to offer the burnt sacrifices of animals as specified by Mosaic Law. *Exodus 27:1 says, "And thou shalt make an altar of shittim wood...".* An altar, in its root, translates from the Hebrew word zabach, meaning to slaughter for sacrifice, slaughter for eating, slaughter for divine judgment, to offer a sacrifice. Under Mosaic Law, there had to be bloodshed to atone for sins. There were multiple types of sacrifices:

- The burnt offering required that the whole animal be consumed. It signified consecration to God and atonement for sins (Exodus 1:1-17).

- The sin/guilt offering reserved part of the offering for the priests. It signified the atonement that would be made by Christ for the remission of sins, thus giving us deliverance from the power and penalty of sin.(Leviticus 5:7-13, Leviticus 6:16-25).

- The peace offering included one offering and required the offerors to eat part of the animal. Christ fulfilled this as our Prince of Peace. Isaiah 53:8 says, "But he was wounded for our transgressions; he was bruised for our iniquities; the chastisement our peace was upon him; and with his stripes we are healed. Christ became our peace offering by granting us salvation" (Leviticus 22:18-25, Leviticus 23:12).

- The meal offerings were offerings that were not animals but were of grain flour or loaves. This included the freewill offerings and the firstfruit offerings. This represents Christ as our firstfruit through His resurrection and second coming. I Corinthians 15:20 and 23 say, "But now Christ is risen from the dead, and become the firstfruits of them that slept…but every man in his own order: Christ the firstfruits; afterward they that are Christ's at his coming" (Leviticus 23:9-14).

The various offerings and sacrifices were established as laws under the Mosaic Covenant and were completed by a required action in the natural. Under the Davidic covenant, the sacrifices were all spiritual, revealing that the law would be fulfilled through Christ. *Jeremiah 33:15 says, "In those days and at that time I will cause the Branch of Righteousness to grow up unto David; and he shall execute judgment and righteousness in the land".* Jesus is the branch of righteousness. The Tabernacle of David represented Christ in the spirit. The physical Tabernacle of David only contained the Ark of the Covenant. It contained the presence of the Lord. The Church (body of Christ) is the spiritual house of the Lord. Kevin J. Conner writes, "Christ is a Son over His house, whose house we are. Both Jew and Gentile are brought ministries established in the Tabernacle of David our worship as empowered by the indwelling Holy Spirit has further revealed that we are houses of the Lord" (The Tabernacle of David).

Instead of burnt sacrifices, the Ministry of Spiritual Sacrifices was instituted by David. *Psalm 27:6 says, "And now shall mine head be lifted up above mine enemies round about me: therefore will I offer in his tabernacle sacrifices of joy; I will sing, yea, I will sing praises unto my God".* The word sacrifice is translated to the Hebrew word zebach, and means to give a thank offering, sacrifices of righteousness, the covenant sacrifice. In this passage, singing praises is a spiritual act that comes from the heart and spirit of man to the Spirit of God. Joy is a fruit of the Holy Spirit. Sacrifices of praise are offered up every day, all day, even today as a part of our daily living. These spiritual sacrifices yield a result of spiritual cleansing.

The Brazen Laver was also the outer court and reflected the Mosiac Law. *Exodus 38:8 says, "And he made the laver of brass, of the looking glasses of the women assembling; which assembled at the door of the tabernacle of the congregation".* The Brazen Laver was a place for washing. The priests had to wash at the Brazen Laver before they could enter into the tabernacle. The basin had mirrors inlaid in the bottom of it, which denoted that the priests were to self-reflect and repent before going inside the tabernacle. The brass or bronze represented judgment. The priests were to judge themselves before entering the tabernacle. The priests were consecrated to the Lord and had to wash themselves, or they would have brought judgment on themselves. This speaks of the lifestyle of holiness that God desires for us to live today.

Ashby and Galan wrote, "Not every pure thing, or person is holy. A common person, or thing can be pure or impure. However, a holy person or thing cannot be holy and impure at the same time" *(Rose Guide to the Tabernacle, p.37).* Jesus is not common; he is holy and has made us holy. Through Jesus' purity, we became pure and holy. *II Corinthians 5:21 says, "For he hath made him to be sin for us, who knew no sin; that we might be made the righteousness of God in him".* Righteousness translates from the Greek word dikaiosyne and means to be in an acceptable condition to God, integrity, virtue, and purity of life, correctness, rightness of thinking, feeling, or acting *(Strong's G1343).* The moment we accept Christ, our conditions change, and we are made right with Him. This washing and consecration is carried out today in water baptism. *Acts 22:16 says, "Why tarriest thou? Arise. And be baptized, and wash away thy sins, calling on the name of the Lord".* In Christ, there is the washing away of sins and the impartation of righteousness.

Jesus is our mediator, intercessor, and High Priest. The High Priest, in the Tabernacle of Moses, was the mediator and intercessor for all of Israel. On the day of atonement, the High Priest went into the Most Holy Place to offer a sacrifice for the sins of man. He had two offerings. One offering was a blood offering because the shedding of blood was required to pay for one's sins. *Leviticus 17:10 says,*

"For the life of the flesh is in the blood: and I have given it to you upon the altar to make an atonement for your souls; for it is the blood that maketh an atonement for the soul".

The word atonement comes from the Hebrew word kaphar and means to cover, purge, make a reconciliation, to pacify, atone for the sins of another person by legal rights *(Strong's H3722)*. Only the High Priest had legal right to enter into the Most Holy Place, and the blood sacrifice was what gave them that legal right. A rite is a ritual that changes an individual's social status *(Wikipedia.com)*. When Jesus gave up his life through his blood, He restored our rite of passage to the presence of God to be in covenant relationship with Him. When we accept Christ, our social status changes from a place of separation and damnation to a place of union with God.

Hebrews 4:14 says, "Seeing then that we have a great High Priest, that is passed into the heavens, Jesus the Son of God, let us hold fast our profession".

Jesus met the requirement for the remission of sins and thrust us into the dispensation of grace. In the Tabernacle of David, there was no longer the activity of the High Priest and of the blood sacrifice. Instead, there was the ministry of praise, rejoicing, and dancing. These acts were spiritual sacrifices to God in replacement of the ritual of animal sacrifice. *I Chronicles 16:10 says, "Glory ye in his holy name: let the heart of them rejoice that seek the Lord".* David established an environment that celebrated the presence of the Lord. We see this in our church services today when we have "praise breaks." These are times in our services to boast about the Lord's greatness. Everyone is in a posture of rejoicing because of the presence of the Lord and out of our love for Him. The word seek comes from the Hebrew word baqash and means to request, to find, or desire. To desire someone speaks of a relationship. David established the ministry of prayer and the principal of relationship. We celebrate those we are in relationship with. The ministries of the Tabernacle of David pointed to the divine relationship those who accept Christ have at the time of salvation.

Jesus, as our High Priest, established this relationship. He says, *"I am the way, the truth, and the life; no man cometh unto the father but by me" (John 14:6).* The New Testament Church currently carries out Christ's ministry as our way through Biblical doctrines and principals. The Tabernacle of Moses carries truths that point to Jesus as the way in the New Testament Church.

Manifestations of the Tabernacle of Moses in the New Testament Church

Jesus as The Way	Representation in the Tabernacle of Moses	New Testament Church Fulfillment (as seen today)	Scriptures
The Way of Approach	The Gate	Repentance and Salvation	Hebrews 6:1,2
The Way of Justification by Faith	The Brazen Alter	Reconciliation and Faith	Hebrews 6;1,2
The Way of Separation & Sanctification	The Brazen Laver	Water Baptism	Acts 2: 38-41, Matt 28: 19-20
The Way of Entrance	The Door The Garment of the Priest	Baptism in the Holy Spirit	Acts 2:4, Luke 20:49
The Way of Illumination	The Golden Lampstand	The Laying on of Hands	Hebrews 6:2
The Way of Communion	The Table of Showbread	Communion	I Corinthians 11:23-24, Matt 26: 26-28
The Way of Prayer, Worship, Intercession	The Altar of Incense	Prayer, Praise, Intercession	Mark 11:17, John 4:24
The Way of Access to the Glory of God	The Veil	The Age of the Kingdom	Hebrews 9:1-10, Hebrews 10:19-22, Hebrews 6:19-20
The Way of Glorification	The Ark of the Covenant	The Finished Redemption and Glorification of the Saints, The Saints Movement	Revelation 21:1-5, Hebrews 6:1-12, Romans 8:26-30

The Tabernacle of David was a tent just like the Tabernacle of Moses, but it did not have the same three sections as the former tabernacle. The dispensation represented through the Tabernacle of David, and its function that operated therein, reveals the progression to the coming dispensation of the Messianic Kingdom and how the people in the Kingdom of God are to function today.

The Tabernacle of David only contained the Ark of the Covenant. There was no Brazen Laver where the priests had to wash before entering into the tabernacle. This is a type of salvation and is already being made clean by Christ and having the grace to access the throne freely. *Romans 5:2 says, "By whom we have access by faith into this grace wherein we stand now stand, and we rejoice in hope of the glory of God".* The Ark of the Covenant and the Most Holy Place was where the glory of God dwelled. The Tabernacle of David was a place to access the glory of God. It was a place of rejoicing.

The Tabernacle of David followed the patterns of God, but the patterns were carried out through worship by the priests and the people rather than through the symbolism of the furniture and rituals carried out by priests within the tabernacle. *II Samuel 6:17 says: And they brought in the Ark of the Lord, and set it in his place, in the midst of the Tabernacle that David has pitched for it: and David offered burnt offerings and peace offerings before the Lord. And soon as David had made an end of offering burnt offerings, he blessed the people in the name of the Lord of Hosts.*

David ended the activity of the burnt offerings, thus marking the transference into the lifestyle of spiritual sacrifices. Both tabernacles carry the patterns of God, but they followed different patterns: the Tabernacle of Moses carried the pattern of God's law, and the Tabernacle of David carried the pattern of grace. David made a final offering and released a blessing, marking the crossover from an old order of priesthood and worship into a new order of priesthood and worship with a deeper intimacy with God.

God in Us

The order of worship David established points to the separation from religion and drawing near to God through a spiritual relationship with Christ. We see this in the progression of Churches throughout history. Churches following the old patterns of worship have a minister in the pulpit and everyone else is below and far away. It is designed so that all the control is given to the pastor, and those holding a high-ranking title—just as the High Priest was the only one with access to the glory zone of the Tabernacle of Moses. There is no establishment of the meaning of Ephesians 4:11 and 12: *"And he gave some apostles; some prophets; and some evangelists; and some, pastors and teachers; for the perfecting of the saints for the work of the ministry, for the edifying of the body of Christ."*

To edify means instruct, uplift, or to enlighten. The Tabernacle of David established the principal of edification through the ministries implemented. Today, we see elements of both the Tabernacle of David and the Tabernacle of Moses in the shadows of our worship services and everyday life in this walk with God. The tabernacles carry significant differences in that one symbolizes the law and the other symbolizes grace. They reflect how the Old and New Testaments and the dispensations of the ages are fulfilled though Christ—the coming of ages.

Supernatural Concepts Applied

The Ark of the Covenant is sometimes referred to as the Ark of the Testimony. When sharing about the power of God, it is important to share our testimony of His goodness to others.

1. *What is your testimony of how God has taken you through dispensations of your life?*

2. *Take time to dance to a song that speaks to your testimony.*

3. *Journal your experience.*

Chapter Four

KINGS AND PRIESTS:
Dancing Your Identity

The new covenant Priesthood establishes us as both kings and priests. To understand our identity and function as New Testament priests, we must explore the Levitical Priesthood as outlined in the Old Testament. The Levitical Priesthood reveals to us our identity in Christ and how we are to carry on the life of Christ as New Testament priests. There is an office and a call. We are to walk in the office of a king as joint heirs with Christ, and we are to fulfill the calling of a priest through servanthood.

Revelation 5:10 says, "And has made us unto our God kings and priests: and we shall reign on the earth". The word king in this passage translates from the Greek word basileus, which means to be leader of the people, prince, commander of the land *(G935)*. Jesus is Kings of Kings and Lord of Lords. He is our leader. As joint heirs with Christ, we are leaders of the people. This speaks not only of a position but of a lifestyle.

Priest in this passage comes from the Greek word heireus and is one who offers sacrifices and in general is busied with sacred rites, a devoted life to Christ. We are a set-aside people who offer sacrifices to the Lord. The Levites were called to live according to the standards that the Lord set for them. They were given charge over the tabernacle itself, as well as the people. The Levites recognized that their life was not their own, but the Lord's. As priests who are called to the sacred dance, we are to offer worship and praise to God. As we walk in the shadow and lineage of Christ by the Holy Ghost, we recognize that our life is not our own. These sacrifices are not limited to our in-house duties but more importantly to our overall living.

We were established as kings through Christ and through the order of Melchizedek. *Genesis 14:18 says, "And Melchizedek king of Salem brought forth bread and wine: and he was the priest of the Most High God".* The name Melchizedek translates from two separate names in Hebrew: Malkiy-Tsedeq and together means "my king is Sedek" *(Strong's H4442).* To get to the true meaning of this name, we have to look at the root meaning of each part of the name. It comes together in sort of a mathematical equation:

Melek: king (Strong's H4428)

+

Tsedeq: justice, righteousness, ruler, of law, of God's attribute, of people enjoying salvation
(Strong's H6664)

=

King of Righteousness

During Biblical times, and even today, names were very much tied to the identity of the person baring the name. Melchizedek was a type of Christ. In this regard, Melchizedek was to be a king who carried God's attributes and upheld justice and righteousness. Jesus is our King who came to execute justice and righteousness. There is a relationship established in the meaning of his name that points to the relationship of God, of Melchizedek, of Christ with us as New Testament priests. By the use of the preposition of, we see that there is a relationship that must be established to belong to the priesthood. By definition, of is used to "express the relationship between a part and a whole and indicates an association between two entities, typically one belonging" *(Googledictionary.com).* Melchizedek was associated with God as both a king and priest. This is parallel to Christ, who is also a king and priest.

In the book, These are the Garments, author C.W. Slemming writes, "Melchizedek had royal blood in his veins; he claimed the title of kingship.... Christ was more than the King of Israel; He too was King of Righteousness. His name was Jehovah Tsidkenu, the Lord our Righteousness" *(p.25 and 26)*. Both parties were associated with God and belonged to God. Melchizedek was both the king and the High Priest of Salem.

Melchizedek walked in both mantles and was a type of our coming Christ who would fulfill both mantles. *Hebrews 7:3 says, "Without father or mother, without descent, having neither beginning of days, nor end of life; but made like unto the Son of God; abideth a priest continually".* There was no record of any priesthood being established before Melchizedek or after. Jesus, likewise, stood alone in his priesthood. Sometimes, as New Testament priests, we will have to stand alone in our priesthood. When we are faced with challenges, when we are faced with decisions that are contrary to the order in which we belong, we must stand. We must remember the office and the call to holiness. Our ability to stand is directly dependent on our attachment to God so that we may continually abide in His presence. We are to remember that we have been made righteous so we don't have to yield to anything except the will of God in our lives.

As New Testament priests, we have the privilege of walking in a dual mantle of kings and priests. *I Peter 2:9 says, "But ye are a chosen generation, a royal priesthood, a holy nation, a peculiar people; that ye should shew forth his praises of him who have called you out of darkness into His marvelous light".* The word priesthood in this passage comes from the Greek word heiretuema and is the office of a priest of the order or body of priests. God calls the body of Christ a body of priests. This means we have direct access to God and are called to be intercessors. This portion of the call is reflected in our prayer life. Every New Testament priest should have a sincere and intense prayer life. Prayer is a constant and consistent communication with God. There are so many facets of prayer that the incense of our prayers can never run out. Just as the priests had to keep the incense burning through prayer and consecration with God.

The word chosen in this passage is the Greek word eklektos, which means to be picked out by God, to elect, to be appointed (to the highest office), choice, the best of its kind, excellence *(Strong's 1588)*. Before the time of salvation, we were predestined to be picked out for excellence. God is excellent, and we are to be a reflection of His excellence. As royal priests, we are not to settle for the mediocrity of common things. This means that we must push ourselves to be the best of our kind at all times. The status quo is unacceptable to us because God has made provision for us to be, do, and have better. When Jesus prayed for the disciples in *John 17:15-16, He said, "I pray not that thou shouldest take them out of the world, but that thou shouldest keep them from the evil. They are not of the world, even as I am not of the world".*

Because we are ambassadors belonging to another kingdom, we are to operate by the kingdom principles not the principles of this world. In the wilderness, the Levites were among the rest of the tribes when they worshiped the golden calf, but they recognized that they were not to do anything lower than the standards God set for His people. They held on to His Word as truth and did not conform to what everyone else was doing. As New Testament priests, we don't conform to what non-believers are doing; rather, we recognize that non-believers are to conform to what God has already established as truth.

In this regard, another truth is revealed about the priesthood. Priests carry the power of influence. During Biblical times, the people knew to take their offerings to the priests so that the priests could give the offerings up to the Lord on their behalf. The Israelites knew that the priests had the ability to influence the spirit realm by the authority that was bestowed upon them by God. We carry this same authority in Christ. For God through Christ has given us keys to the kingdom:

"And I will give you the keys to the Kingdom of Heaven: whatsoever thou shalt bind on earth shall be bound in Heaven: whatsoever thou shalt loose on earth shall be loosed in Heaven" (Matt 16:19)

In the tabernacle, only the priest carried the keys so only the priests had access to enter into the Holy Place and the Most Holy Place, which was reserved for the High Priest. Then Christ came and gave everyone who believes the keys. We are to influence the atmosphere within us, first and around us in any worship setting. We have the power in Christ and the Holy Spirit to minister dances that bind and dances that loose.

Both a king and priest speak of sonship. A king is usually succeeded by His son—the prince. Under the Aaronic Priesthood, Aaron and his sons were permitted to serve in the tabernacle. The rite of passage into the priesthood was sonship. *Exodus 28:1 says, "And take thou now unto thee Aaron thy brother, and his sons with him, from among the children of Israel, that he may minister unto me in the priest's office…"*.

This office was reserved for Aaron and his sons; going forward the priests had to be a part of the lineage of Aaron. The purpose of the priesthood was also revealed in this passage as well. We are to serve the Lord first then rule as kings through the dance. We cannot enjoy the fullness of rulership without first serving the ministering to God. Having a lifestyle of worship with and for God is to be the beginning and ending of our dance. We are to serve the Lord out of our relationship with Him and our love for Him. We must learn to take care of the holy things before we can effectively carry out the mandates of the Kingdom through dance.

It was the responsibility of the Levites to take care of the holy things pertaining to the Lord and the tabernacles. Numbers 3:7, 8 says:

And they shall keep his charge, and the charge of the whole congregation before the tabernacle of the congregation, to do the service of the tabernacle. And they shall keep all the instruments of the tabernacle of the congregation, and the charge of the children of Israel, to do the service of the tabernacle.

The word charge in this passage comes from the Hebrew word

mishmereth and means to guard, a function or obligation, a ceremonial office, to preserve *(H4931)*. The priests had the obligation to serve in a ceremonial office that preserved the holiness of the tabernacle of God. God was very specific about who could draw near to Him and how they were to draw near to him.

As priests living under the New Testament covenant, we are to preserve the holiness of the Kingdom through the tabernacle of our bodies. We may not live in such a way that does not honor God then go before Him and His people to minister in dance or any other service that we may be called to. A lifestyle of rebellion and defiance will not be tolerated by God as it is considered strange fire. Two of Aaron's sons offered strange fire to the Lord, and scripture says they were devoured by fire sent from the Lord (*Leviticus 10: 1-2*). We must allow God to devour with His fire anything that is in our lives that would be presented before him as strange fire. Once we repent or change our minds and hearts towards these things, we must not return to those ways, persons, places, etc. Walking in the office of a priest is not to be taken lightly. It is more than just a position that comes with a lineage as seen with Nadab and Abihu. We cannot, by any means, take on an attitude of entitlement. Rather, we are to take on an attitude of responsibility and humility.

The incense that was commanded by God to be used in the tabernacle was made of "sweet spices, stacte, and onycha, and galbanum; these sweet with pure frankincense" (*Exodus 30:34*). Each one was a type of Christ's ministry as our great High Priest, and in turn is to become our reflection as New Testament priests. It is important to note that the ingredients used to make the incense had to be crushed in order to be used. This means that everything that is of self has to be crushed in order for us to truly be used of God; in order to truly reflect the identity of God on Earth, we have to allow any self-made identity to be crushed and taken away.

The requirements of the incense reveal key requirements of our worship:

- It was to be sweet, as Christ's ministry was filled with sweetness (*Song of Solomon 5:16*).

- It was to be pure, as Christ was Pure (*Hebrews 7:26*).

- It was to be holy, as Christ ministered in absolute Holiness and sinless-ness (*I John 2:1 and Hebrews 7:26*).

- It was to be perpetual, as Christ ministers in the power of an endless life. He is ever living to make intercession for us. He's an everlasting Savior *(Hebrews 7:25, Ephesians 6:18, Colossians 4:2 and Revelations 8:3)*.

- It was to be a perfume as Christ was fragrant in His whole being. (*Ephesians 5:2*).

This reveals a truth about was the Old Testament priest before they were called priests and even once they were called priests; they went through a process of crushing, and anything that was not sweet, pure, holy, perpetual, or perfume was removed from within their heart and character so they may minister before God. One can imagine that the priests must have carried this aroma of God on their clothes so that a person knew when they had been in the presence of God when they came in contact with the priests.

This beautiful fragrance speaks to the New Testament priest—the sincerity of our worship as a ministry and a lifestyle must carry the same characteristics of the ingredients of the incense as well as the character and ministry of Christ. We too must allow anything that is not pure, sweet, holy, perpetual, or perfume to be crushed out of our hearts and minds so that when we minister in dance, a sweet aroma is lifted unto God. If we do not allow God to crush these areas, then the true ministry of the dance will not be released through us, and the true office of the New Priest will not be carried out. We must allow God to have ALL of our whole being by drawing near to Him. The crushing is a process designed that we may draw near to Him.

The Lord made it very clear that strangers were not to draw near to him. *Numbers 3:10 says, "And thou shalt appoint Aaron and His sons, and they shall wait on their priest's office: and the stranger that cometh nigh shall be put to death".*

Anyone who was not appointed to be close to, or in the direct presence of, God would die. The lives that priests were to live identified them as persons who, by right and by rite, could go into the presence of God. Some of the Levites lost their honor as a priest by not upholding God's mandates for the priesthood. Some of the Levites rebelled with the children of Israel when they worshiped idols. God's reply was, " *Thus saith the Lord God; No stranger, uncircumcised in heart, nor uncircumcised in the flesh, shall enter into my sanctuary, of any stranger that is among the children of Israel" (Ezekiel 44:9)*.

One of the definitions of a stranger is a person who is unacquainted with or unaccustomed to something; a person who is not member of a family, group, community, or the like as a visitor or guest *(Dictionary.com)*. The Levites were to be acquainted with God and remain acquainted with God throughout their lives as servants. Their disobedience caused them to be unacquainted with God. As a result, distance was put between God and them. They were no longer allowed to come into the holy place or the most holy place. Their duties then were kept within the confines of the outer court, the gates, and the sanctuary.

As New Testament priests, we are to acquaint ourselves with God and remain acquainted with God throughout our entire lives. We acquaint ourselves with God by studying scripture, praying, worshiping, serving, having a fellowship with God, tithing, etc. These are some of the ways that we draw near to God. Just as we spend time with our natural family, we are to spend time with

God—before we set foot to minister in dance. It is out of this divine acquaintance that our worship and dance is birthed.

Effective Not Defective

Among other requirements set forth to be qualified as a priests in *Leviticus 21:16-21*, one was that they could not have any physical defects the Lord listed. These same requirements are applicable to the spiritual condition of New Testament priest today. The term priest refers to our function as servants in, to, and for the Kingdom of God. Priests were rendered defective and unable to carry out the call if they had any physical defects. Likewise, we cannot carry any spiritual defects because it would render us to be ineffective and hinder our ability to carry out our assignment.

Leviticus 21:18 also lists several defects. They each have a spiritual meaning to the New Testament priest:

> Flat nose; lacking perspective, shallow, lacking possibility of change *(English Definition Dictionary, reverso.com)*

A flat-nosed person is a person who lacks discernment and cannot receive or dig into the deep places of truth in God because they are too shallow to receive wisdom. A flat nose leads to being stiff-necked and resistant to change, which will cause this type of person to miss the moves of God. The priests had to be ready to transport the Ark of the Covenant. It took wisdom to know when and how to accomplish this task. It also required that they paid attention to their leader and God so that they knew when to move. As New Testament priests, we are to pay attention to our prochorus (leader of the dance and chief choreographer) so that we know when to dance and when not to dance, and how to adjust the ministry as God gives new visions.

Acts 7:51: "Ye stiff-necked and uncircumcised in heart and ears, ye do always resist the Holy Ghost, as our fathers did, so do ye."

Proverbs 29:1: "He, that being often reproved hardeneth his neck, shall suddenly be destroyed, and that without remedy."

> Superfluous Sara *(H8311)* - Stretched out; a person who has a member (especially the ear) that is stretched out too long.

A superfluous person is a person who lacks balance. They do not remain in step with the Holy Spirit as they tend to move ahead or too far behind God. This speaks of lack of submission to authority because they oftentimes have trouble remaining in step or in rank as their walk is out of balance with God, their leader, or the rest of the team. This person has the inability to follow directions. The priests in the Old Testament had to follow every directive from Moses so that they completed their priestly assignments in the tabernacle. We must learn to be able to follow the directives as given to us by anyone who is in authority over us.

Proverbs 8:33: "Hear instruction be wise, And do not neglect it."

Proverbs 16:20: "Those who listen to instruction will prosper; those who trust the Lord will be happy."

> Broken footed or broken handed,- sheber *(H7667)*; a person who has a breach, fracture, or break.

This person lacks the ability to trust or be trusted. They are prone to breach a confidence or break a bond of trust which leads to destruction. This also speaks of the lack of a heart postured in servanthood because the person with a broken hand has the inability to give. The Levitical priests had to be trustworthy in order to serve in the tabernacle. They were entrusted with taking care of holy things.

The broken foot leaves the inability to go and do the work of a servant. This was and still is the overall assignment of the priesthood - to serve.

Proverbs 28:26- A gossip betrays a confidence, but a trustworthy man keeps a secret.

John 13:14 "If I then, your Lord and Master, have washed your feet; ye also ought to wash one another's feet."

> Crookbackt - gibben *(H1384)*; humpbacked/hunchback-curving of the spine that causes a bowing of the back. *(Wikipedia.com)*

This speaks of a person who lacks integrity. They may appear one way but will bow at anything to fit in. There is a lack of uprightness in the heart. As New Testament priests it is vital that we are who we say we are. In the Book of Daniel King Nebuchadnezzar built a golden image and set a decree that all were to bow to this golden image. The Shadrach, Meshach, and Abed-Nego refused and boldly declared, even at the threat of death, that they would not bow to the golden image. They were known for their skill and excellence as they were as just as the noble Daniel. They upheld their integrity as noble Jewish citizens by not bowing to the golden image, which was something that they knew was forbidden, according to their law. They hid the law in their heart and when their integrity was challenged, they pulled on their faith. A New Testament priest's integrity will be challenged, but we must pull on our faith, which is built by what is hidden in our heart. Integrity is the result of outward actions driven by what's within. A person who lacks integrity will reveal what isn't inside of them during such tests.

Daniel 3:17, 18: "If it be so, our God whom we serve is able to deliver us from the burning fiery furnace, and he will deliver us out of thine hand, O king. But if not, be it known unto thee, O king that we will not serve thy gods, nor worship the golden image in which though has set up."

> Dwarf, daq *(H1851)* - thin, small, fine, gaunt; halfling *(Wikipedia.com)*.

This person lacks the ability to grow. This speaks of a person who is immature and unteachable as they only grow to be half and remain half of their God-intended size. In this regard, this person lacks the ability to yield to God so that they can grow. When we are driving and we see a yield sign, we know to give way for another car to pass. In order to be able to grow in God, we must give way of self so that God can pass through us. The priests had to be 25 years old in order to serve in the tabernacle. This speaks of maturity. From the age of 25 until age 30, the Levites were trained, then released to serve. The age of the Levites spoke of maturity in the training process, which speaks of their ability to yield to God for what He wanted to do through them in the next season of their lives as priests.

Ephesians 1:17 "That the God of our Lord Jesus Christ, the Father of Glory, may give to you the spirit of wisdom and revelation in the knowledge of Him. The eyes of you understanding being enlightened; that ye may know what is the hope of his calling, and the riches of the glory of his inheritance in the saints."

II Timothy 2:15 "Study to shew thyself approved unto God, a workman that needeth not be ashamed, rightly dividing the word of truth."

Blemish in the eye, teballul *(H8400)* – obscurity, defect; confusion, having stains or spotted

Ayin *(H5869)* - physical eye, showing mental qualities, mental faculties

This person has an un-renewed mind, causing confusion in their vision, and the desire to separate from sin is not present in this individual. This means that there is not enough time spent studying God's Word as the mind is renewed by the washing of the Word. If a person has not renewed their mind towards sin and life altogether, then they will not be able to walk in the purity that Christ established for us. A blemish in the eye, in this regard, also speaks of lack of revelation by the Holy Spirit. New Testament priests MUST spend time in the Word of God with the Holy Spirit in order to receive revelation. Without revelation, we are unable to live out the Word of God, let alone release the Word of God through dance.

Ephesians 1:17: "That the God of our Lord Jesus Christ, the Father of Glory, may give to you the spirit of wisdom and revelation in the knowledge of Him. The eyes of you understanding being enlightened; that ye may know what is the hope of his calling, and the riches of the glory of his inheritance in the saints."

Luke 11:34: "The light of the body is the eye: therefore when thine eye is single, thy whole body also is full of light; but when thine eye is evil, thy bod also is full of darkness."

Scurvy or scabbed, garab *(H1618)* - to itch, scab

Yallepheth *(H3217)* - scab, skin sore, an eruptive disease; impetigo, blisters, eczema

A scurvy or scabbed person is a person who lacks self-control. *Galatians 5* lists self-control and patience as two of the nine fruits of the Spirit. A person who has scurvy or is scabbed is often irritable, un-loving, and shows erratic behavior, i.e. they are quick-tempered with a sharp tongue or lack discipline and patience. In the ministry of deliverance, eczema is sometimes identified as a sign that a person is under a curse. To be quick-tongued and quick-tempered gives people the propensity to speak curses and not blessings. *James 3:1-12* shares wisdom on why it is important to learn to control one's tongue. To adopt this principle also will aid in learning to control one's temper and build patience.

The Old Testament priests had the responsibility of placing the sin offering on the Brazen Altar. We can be for certain that this was done with an attitude of compassion not anger. Compassion was what was in God's heart when He sent Christ to atone for our sins. That same compassion was what was in Jesus' heart as He was walking and crawling, carrying our sins with him on the cross at Calvary. New Testament priests are to carry this same posture of compassion for the lost, the hurting, and even those who are believers who might be struggling in an area. Scripture tells us to bear each other's burdens not spaz out in judgment.

Galatians 6:2: "Bear ye one another's burdens, and so fulfill the law of Christ."

Galatians 5:22-23: "But the fruit of the spirit is love, joy, peace, longsuffering [patience], gentleness, goodness, faith, meekness, temperance [self-control]: against such there is no law."

James 3: 9, 10 "Therewith we bless God, even the Father; and therewith curse us men, which are made after the similitude of God. Out of the same mouth proceeded blessings and cursing. My brethren, these things ought not so to be."

Has his stones broken, eshek *(H810)* - testicle, stone

Merowach *(H4790)* - castrated, bruised, crushed, rub, dubious (doubting, suspicious, hesitant, unsure)

A person with crushed stones speaks of a person who lacks boldness due to unbelief. The reason why the Levites were chosen as the priesthood was because they believed God and showed it through their actions. They boldly stood for what was right and boldly opted not to participate in idol worship. They had the courage to say no to what they believed was against God's will.

The enemy through the temptation of disobedience was not allowed to castrate their destiny. In the natural, a synonym for castrate is neuter. To neuter a male animal causes them to be infertile, or unable to reproduce. The Old Testament priests were to come from the lineage of Aaron. This means they had to reproduce after themselves. A person who has "broken stones" cannot reproduce after Christ because they lack the boldness and faith to share the gospel. God is faithful, creative, and fruitful. His priests we are called to be producers—birthing more of the Kingdom onto the Earth. This is a type of the re-birth that is to occur during the dispensation of the Messianic Age (*Isaiah 66:9-12*).

Joshua 1:9: "Have I not commanded you be strong and courageous. Do not be afraid; do not be discouraged, for the Lord your God will be with you wherever you go" (NIV).

II Corinthians 3:12: "Therefore since we have such a hope, we are very bold" (NIV).

Isaiah 66:9, 10: "Shall I bring to the birth and not cause to bring forth? Saith the Lord: shall I cause to bring forth and shut the womb? Saith God. Rejoice ye with Jerusalem and be glad all that love her rejoice for joy all ye that mourn for her."

Unlike the Levites from the Aaronic Priesthood, we have a grace card that was issued to us by Christ. There is still, however, a call to holiness that must be upheld by New Testament priests. Paul says, in Romans 6:1-2, "What shall we say then? Shall we continue in sin, that grace may abound? God Forbid. How shall we that are dead to sin, live any longer therein?" Through the work of the cross, we are strangers to sin, and we are able to draw near to God. As we honor and reverence even the third person of the God-head—the Holy Spirit living inside of us—we can walk in authority over sin. This means that we will uphold standards of purity and integrity.

The Levites were called out by the Lord to be priests because of their commitment to obey God. *Deuteronomy 33:9 says, "Who said unto his father and to his mother, I have not seen him; neither did he acknowledge his brethren, nor knew his own children: for they have observed thy word and kept thy covenant".* When Israel sinned against God and built the golden calf, the Levites refused and upheld the covenant they had with God. Even while everyone else was doing wrong, the Levites did what was right in the eyes of the Lord.

Nothing came between them and their commitment to God. *Exodus 32:26 says, "Then Moses stood in the gate of the camp, and said, who is on the Lord's side? Let him come unto to me. And all the sons of Levi gathered themselves unto him".* The Levites showed loyalty and faithfulness to God by choosing not to participate with the rest of Israel. As New Testament priests, we are to choose not to participate in the activities of the world that do not bring honor to God. We are to choose to live consecrated lives in loyalty to God. This means we have to dare to be different.

We are to mirror *I Peter 1:15, 16, which says, "But as he which has called you is holy, so be ye holy in all manner of conversation: Because it is written be ye holy; for I am holy".* The word holy in this passage originates from the Greek word hagios and means most holy thing or a saint *(Strong's G40)*. God calls us as His children a most holy thing. The priesthood was exclusive to Aaron and his sons. As sons of God, we carry an exclusive holiness. Once we take on the mindset and posture of the divine fact that we have been made holy, our lives will begin to reflect holiness. Upon accepting the call to minister in sacred dance or priestly worship, we must seek God for the revelation of holiness, as it dwells in partnership with the ministry itself. Under the Davidic order, the ministry of dancing was established and carried out by the priesthood. We have been made holy by Christ, and the Holy Spirit lives inside of us, thus sealing us to holiness. The Holy Spirit is to live through us. As we are led by His Spirit, we must uphold holy standards by living holy lives.

Ezekiel 44:15 says, "The priests the Levites, the Sons of Zadok, that kept the charge of my sanctuary when the children of Israel went astray from they shall come near to me to minister unto me, and they shall stand before me to offer unto me the fat and the blood, saith the Lord God." Zadok upheld his integrity and remained in obedience even while others around him were doing wrong. His faithfulness to God and His character caused God to react in His Faithful, and Zadok and his descendants were elevated. They were privileged to be able to come near to God in the Most Holy Place. Christ came so that we would be able to come near to God in the Most Holy Place of our spirit. We are to enter into this place of intimacy and honor the charge, which in our case is the dance and ministry of movement. We carry out this responsibility by:

- sharpening our skills as dancers (taking classes, attending workshops and trainings),

- taking a stand to honor God and the revelation that He has given us,

- serving by helping other dancers and dance teams,

- being accountable to leadership in our local fellowship,

- carrying on the vision for our house,

- being on our post during assigned times of worship, and

- having consistent attendance at designated times for trainings, rehearsals, and meetings.

The Bible goes into great detail about the responsibilities of the priests. The priests served in the tabernacle on behalf of their whole nation. They recognized that they were a part representing a whole. One of the assignments of the Levitical Priests was to minister to the people. *Romans 12:10 says, "Be kindly affectioned one to another with brotherly love in honour preferring one another."* Honour in this passage refers to a valuing by which the price is fixed, the price paid or received for a person or a thing bought or sold. It also refers to the honor given to a superior due to rank or office. Its meaning in root comes from the Greek word time which means to pay, recompense; to pay penalty or suffer punishment *(Strong's G5099).*

The Old Testament priests had the responsibility of offering sacrifices to God on behalf of the people for their sins. They served as intercessors or mediators between man and God. Typically, one would think that the people of Israel would honor the priests because they were of such a high-ranking position of authority, but contrariwise, the priests honored God, the people, and themselves. The priests walked in honor because they had the understanding of the fixed price for sin, which was death. As New Testament priests we are to honor God, our people, and ourselves by walking in the understanding that the price for our lives and freedom from the punishment and penalty of sin has already been paid by our Lord Jesus Christ. As priests of the dance, we are to represent and release this truth when we minister in dance as well as in our everyday living.

A Reflection of God's Beauty

The priesthood, for the new covenant priest, is a mindset—another facet that the Lord has established as a part of our identity. Our garments reflect our identity in Him as well. They are an outer reflection of an inward call. Our garments reflect who we are in the body. In this regard, even our garments serve as a reflection of our identity. This is why it is important not to copy someone else's garments. Team garments are an exception, but again, they reflect the function and call of the ministry team who wears them. Our garments are a reflection of the office that God has called us to live out of as priests. Christ is our garment, and He has covered us with dignity.

Each portion of the priestly garments speaks to a portion of the call of the New Testament priests. *Exodus 39:27 says, "And they made coats of fine linen of woven work for Aaron and his sons."* The tunic was to be a foundation for the High Priests. It was the basic garment of the priests. It speaks to the holiness that must be upheld by the new covenant priesthood. C.W. Slemming wrote, "In these particular garments the High Priest and other priests were alike, for all wore the white tunic with this one difference: it was the High Priest's undergarment, but the priest it was his outer garment" *(p.37)*.

Christ is righteousness and has clothed us in righteousness. *Revelation 19:8 says, "It was given to her to clothe herself in fine linen, bright and clean; for the fine linen is the righteous acts of the saints"*

(NIV). As brides of Christ, we have a foundation of righteousness and purity. He has presented us pure before the Lord. In the natural, our garments are to be kept clean, and we are to always make sure we have proper foundation garments. In the spirit, this means that we are to always have a strong foundation in the Word of God, as scripture is to be the foundation of all we do, including the dance.

The robe of Aaron's priestly garment speaks to the dignity and authority that we have in Christ. *Exodus 28:31, 35 says, "And thou shalt make the robe of the Ephod all blue...And beneath upon the hem of it thou shalt make pomegranates of blue, and of purple, and of scarlet, round about the hem thereof: and bells of gold between them round about"*. This was the first time the word robe was mentioned in scripture. In Hebrew, robe is the word ma'iyl and is a garment worn over a tunic by men of rank, a long garment of the High Priest, and was worn by David's daughters *(Strong's 4598)*. It's meaning in root is to act unfaithfully or treacherously, to transgress, against man, against God, against a devoted thing, or against one's husband *(Strong's H4603)*.

The robe was worn by men of rank to show their power and faithfulness to their call. In this regard, the robe represents the priests' discipline to abstain from treacherous activities dishonorable to God, Himself, or those that he served. As New Testament priests, we are to be disciplined in the authority and by the authority given to us by God. C. W. Slemming states, "Every servant of the Lord who ministers in holy things should himself respect his office and should be respected because of his office" *(These are the Garments, p. 42)*. The more we know about our office and our call, the more we become disciplined in the holy things, resulting in respect and honor.

The pomegranates and bells speak to the New Testament priest as well. The bells represent the sound of Heaven and the Great Commission to share the gospel. *Ephesians 6:15 says, "And your feet shod with the preparation of the gospel of peace."*. The bells are a symbol of peace. The gospel is that Christ our Savior has made us at peace with God as our Prince of Peace. We are to carry this message in our hearts and release this message when we dance. The pomegranates are a type of the fruit of the spirit and thus points to the indwelling of the Holy Spirit who is to work through us as we serve. Through proper use of holy garments, we as Kingdom priests are stating, *"I am crucified with Christ: nevertheless I live yet not I, but Christ liveth in me: and the life I now live in the flesh I live by the faith of the Son of God, who loved me and gave himself for me" (Galatians 2:20)*. As we represent Christ on the Earth as New Testament priests, we are to keep in mind the death of our flesh so that we may give of ourselves to serve others.

Exodus 28:6 says, "And they shall make the Ephod of gold, of blue, of purple, of scarlet, and fine twined linen, with cunning work... And thou shall take two onyx stones, and grave on them the names of the children of Israel". The colors of the Ephod typified the power of Christ and the stones typified the burden (us and our sins) that he would take to the cross. *Galatians 6:2 says, "Bear ye one another's burdens and thereby fulfill the law of Christ"*. We are to support one another as fellow priests.

The way the colors of the Ephod come together speaks to the unity of faith. Gold represents the Deity of God and His Divine Nature. Blue represents the Divinity of Christ, the Kingdom, and the Holy Spirit. Red is the color of man, as well as the blood atonement. Purple speaks to a combination of the two colors, red and blue, and reveals the royalty and kingship that we currently have in Christ. Heaven came to Earth in the form of man to manifest kingship and dominion on the Earth by the divine power of God. All of the colors come together to represent the trinity and the establishment of our relationship to the trinity.

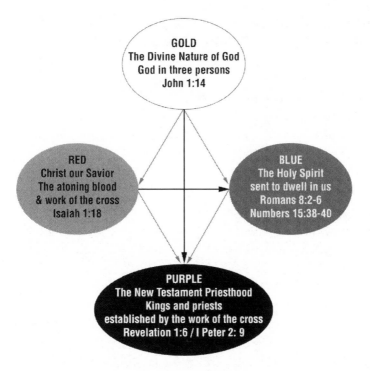

The diagram above reveals that the assignment of the Old Testament priest was to carry the burdens of the priest before God, and that God bestowed power and authority on the priest. Once Jesus came, He bestowed power and authority in the New Testament priest. We are to carry out this mantle in the ministries we are assigned to. When we connect all of the colors, we see triangles, which are indicative of our triune God. We also see the cross, which is where Christ established the New Testament priest. *I Peter 3:18 says, "For Christ also hath once suffered for sins, the just for the unjust, that he might bring us to God, being put to death in the flesh, but quickened by the Spirit"*. The way the colors come together speaks to the unity of faith.

The breastplate also speaks of unity of faith. *Exodus 28:15 says, "And thou shall make the breastplate of judgment with cunning work; after the work of the Ephod though shall make it; of gold, of blue, and of purple and of scarlet... And thou shalt set in it stones, even four rows of stones"*). The breastplate to the New Testament priest typifies the

Church and the unity of our individual gifts. All of the stones were different from one another, but they each served a purpose to the priest.

All of us are precious jewels in God's sight. There is to be no competition in ministry. *I Corinthians 12:12 says, "For as the body is one, and hath many members, and all the members of that one body, being many, are one body: so also is Christ. We are all to work together"* (NLT). The stones then reveal the individual tribes coming together as one nation. We may belong to different local fellowships and reside in different regions, but we are all to come together for the same purpose—to exalt our King by advancing the Kingdom. The breastplate also reveals the righteousness that we have in Christ.

Ephesians 6:14 tells us to "have on the breastplate of righteousness". In the natural, the breastplate was worn during battle to protect the heart of the soldier. Together, the New Testament priests form a breastplate that protects the heart of worship. This is why we are to operate as one with our Minister of music and other ministries that affect worship services.

Aaron, as the High Priest, and *Exodus 28:2 says, "And thou shalt make holy garments for glory and for beauty".* We are called to be holy and to reveal the glory and beauty of the Lord. Holy in this passage is the Hebrew word qodesh and means apartness, sacredness; of God, of people, of things *(Strong's H6944)*. Just as we are called to be holy, so are our garments. This means that as Kingdom priests, the garments that we wear for ministry are to be consecrated for that use and purpose only. They cannot be worn as everyday apparel.

The priests had specific consecrated use of their garments and could not mix them with what was common. *Ezekiel 42:14 says, "When the priests enter therein, then shall they not go out of the holy place into the utter court, but there they should lay their garments wherein they minister; for they are holy; and shall put on other garment, and shall put on other garments, and shall approach to those things which are for the people".* Growing up, my siblings and I had specific clothes that we wore during specific times. We had regular clothes, play clothes, and church clothes. We were not allowed to play outside in our church clothes, and we were not allowed to wear our play clothes to church. Even within the priesthood of dance, there are specific garments that are to be worn to teach in (equipping garments), to minister dance in, and for rehearsals and classes. Just as our garments represent the anointing of God, they also carry the anointing of God on them. The priests spent the majority of their time in the tabernacle causing the smells and residue of the worship activity that went on in the tabernacle to remain and be carried on their garments. As we worship with sincere pure hearts and spend time in the presence of the Lord, our garments also carry the residue of our inner personal worship.

Our garments identify us as priests. If we were to travel to foreign countries, we would see that most cultures wear attire that is specific to that country. Take India, for example. There are garments that are worn as everyday wear, garments that are worn among a specific caste group, and garments that are worn specifically for festivals. These various garments share the same premise that they are to represent the culture and heritage of India. India is known for their beautifully crafted sarees and Anakarli kameez with bright and beautiful colors. As New Testament priests, our garments represent the culture of the Kingdom and the heritage of the priesthood. What our garments represent, and who they represent, is interpreted by how they are made, by the colors, when they are worn, and how they are worn.

Psalm 104:2 says, "Who coverest thyself with light as with a garment...". This passage reveals the importance of being covered. We are not to wear garments that are revealing. In the manual, Make His Praise Glorious, Dr. Pamela Hardy writes, "To God garments and light are synonymous. In garment design, we seek to clothe ourselves with truth" *(p.90)*. Our garments are to reveal the truth of who God is and in turn speaks to the truth of who we are as priests. Light is how the natural eye interprets colors and images. If the eye is unable to receive proper amounts of light, then the perception of images are off. In the spirit, we interpret colors and images by the light and truth of God's Word and the Holy Spirit. As New Testament priests, we are to make sure that our garments properly convey messages of truth, holiness, salvation, and love.

The New Testament priesthood is the manifestation of the restoration of the Old Testament priesthood under a new and better covenant. We are to seek God continually to go forth as light bearers on the Earth. *Hebrews 8:6 says, "But now hath he obtained a more excellent ministry, by how much also he is the mediator of a better covenant, which was established upon better promises".* Let in the identity and character of our High Priest, Christ Jesus.

Supernatural Concepts Applied

1. *Review the section on the character of the priesthood. Write down any areas of your life that may need to be adjusted so that you may fully serve God and His Kingdom.*

2. *Think about your favorite color. Do you own any garments in that color? How does that garment reflect your identity as a servant of the Lord?*

3. *Take time every day to pray on your armour as outlined in Ephesians. Record your experiences.*

Part Two

Introduction to Dances of the Supernatural

The supernatural is the ability to depart from what is considered normal or usual and comes with the result of transcending beyond the laws of nature. The supernatural originated with God, and belongs to God. The enemy has created a counterfeit version of the supernatural, which is why the supernatural is misconceived to be magic or witchcraft. I believe that God is redeeming the Church (the body of Christ) back to its original function, purpose, and divine identity—the supernatural, God-given identity.

The way to do this is to believe that God still operates in miracles and to understand how to connect with Heaven. Instead of existing in the presence of God, we have been given special access to ascend in worship and descend in the supernatural power of God. As we adopt this paradigm, the dance is transformed into a vehicle that God can use to win souls, heal all manner of disease, and proclaim the good news of the Kingdom of Heaven.

Jacob left Beersheba and set out for Harran. When he reached a certain place, he stopped for the night because the sun had set. Taking one of the stones there, he put it under his head and lay down to sleep. He had a dream in which he saw a stairway resting on the earth, with its top reaching to Heaven, and the angels of God were ascending and descending on it. (Genesis 28:10, 11 NLT)

The angels in Jacob's dream were ascending and descending. They were going up and down the ladder, meaning they were bringing things from Heaven to the Earth. We see a pattern here that Heaven is open to us. If we are able to believe and see it, then we are able to access, or enter into, the Heavenly places to procure what we need to release it back onto the Earth. This is why Jesus told us to pray. *"Thy will be done on earth as it is in heaven ,* (Matthew 6:10). We are to seek to implement the culture of the Kingdom of Heaven on the Earth. The culture of the Kingdom is the healing, deliverance, love, peace, and joy in the Holy Spirit.

The Lord desires to open the Heaven's over us, and pour out blessings and favor. *Isaiah 45:8 says, "Open up, O heavens, and pour out your righteousness. Let the earth open wide so salvation and righteousness can sprout up together. I, the LORD, created them"* (NLT). The Lord created everything that was made. He created the supernatural, and when He created humankind (you and me), He had the supernatural in mind. The Bible declares that we are made in His image and likeness. This is why He sent the Holy Spirit to live inside of us to help us so that we would be able to operate in Him through the supernatural power of God.

Dances of the supernatural create a way of thinking and living operating independently of mere dance technique. This is the place where dance and the power of God converge. When something converges, it meets at a point and crosses over. The Lord is calling for us not just to dance but to cross over into the glory realm. That is the power of God called the supernatural.

The Lord wants us to embrace the supernatural as our normal, knowing that nothing is impossible because the "I AM" is possible. He says that nothing is impossible because He is possible. I am sending you to an unlimited place. As you meditate on this truth, begin to see anew. Begin to see finances unlimited, miracles unlimited, healing unlimited, revelation unlimited, peace unlimited, and love unlimited. There are no limits in the supernatural power of God.

Your access is NOW! God will show you the codes, keys, and combinations that will unlock unlimited provision and unlimited access! Don't look for resources—use your keys and become the resource! Be encouraged to fully embrace the supernatural. *Matthew 9:29 says, "Then he touched their eyes and said, "Because of your faith, it will happen".* Your ability to function in the supernatural power of God is directly attached to your measure of faith.

This portion of your study is a journey into the supernatural power of God and will explore how the supernatural manifests through the believer. Seek to apply these truths to your dance ministry as you are serving through the Kingdom Arts.

Access granted!

Chapter Five

SEE AGAIN!
BELIEVE AGAIN!

We are experiencing a time of Kingdom restoration. God is bringing life to things that were once barren. For some, He is restoring our voice; for others, He is restoring our hope back into our function under our true identity. Proper order is being restored to the Kingdom.

Joel 2:25 says: *I will repay you for the years the locusts have eaten-- the great locust and the young locust, the other locusts and the locust swarm -- my great army that I sent among you. You will have plenty to eat and be satisfied And praise the name of the LORD your God, Who has dealt wondrously with you; Then My people will never be put to shame.*

Your days of devastation, turmoil, frustration, anguish, and disappointment are over. Restoration is here—NOW! Now is the time for the true worshipers—those who worship in spirit and in truth—to SEE AGAIN, DREAM AGAIN, BELIEVE AGAIN!

Receive New Sight!

To function in the supernatural, we must be able to see that the supernatural is available to us. To see means to perceive with the eyes or to discern visually; to deduce mentally after reflection or from information. God is restoring sight not only to the physically blind but also to the spiritually blind because we must be able to see clearly in order to function in the supernatural dimension. We will only be able to apprehend that which we can see. This means that the ability to function in the supernatural is directly dependent upon our level of revelation of the Word and will of God.

Matthew 6:22 says, "The light of the body is the eye; therefore if thine eye be single, thy whole body shall be full of light". In the natural, the eye interprets what we see by how we receive light. Light, in the spirit, refers to goodness over evil, being led by God, understanding, purity, and the glory of God. We must live a lifestyle that is full of light so that the supernatural is our normal. We will not see the supernatural if we cannot see spiritually. In this regard, we must also desire revelation while living a holy life. The supernatural does not work when we try to use mere head knowledge because God does not manifest Himself within the confines of human reason. We must depend on the revealed knowledge that can only come from God.

It is important to see by the illumination of God's Word because His light dispels all darkness. Proper sight helps us to discern the difference between good and evil. *I Timothy 4:1 says, "Now the Holy Spirit tells us clearly that in the last times some will turn away from the true faith; they will follow deceptive spirits and teachings that come from demons."* We must be able to see because there is a warfare on the eyes that seeks to deceive God's people, causing them to be trapped in spiritual blindness. It is important to note that the opposite of the supernatural is witchcraft. This is why we must depend on God and not any strength of our own. WE must be able to see because there is a direct counterfeit of God's supernatural power—the power of the devil.

I Peter 5:8 says, "Be sober, be vigilant; because your adversary the devil walks about like a roaring lion, seeking whom he may devour". In other words, be alert. We have to be alert because as Kingdom agents, we have to be prepared at all times to minister to others in the Kingdom. We must be prepared servants of the Lord. Being alert means that we have to keep our eyes open and focused. Keen eyesight is needed to be able to see our enemies from afar.

See again to be prepared for battle. The Bible tells us to watch and pray. We must watch so that we may wage war offensively—not waiting for the battle to come to us. See and engage in the battle!

God is increasing our ability to see. He is giving us new vision just like He gave to Saul who was later named Paul. *Acts 22:12a, 13 reads, "And one Ananias came unto me…and stood and said Brother Saul, receive thy sight. And the same hour I looked upon him".* Paul was blind in the natural and had his natural sight restored. However, this reveals that he was also spiritually blind to the things of the Kingdom. His sight had to be restored in order to take his position in the Kingdom. Having new sight puts us in position to execute the Kingdom on the Earth. God no longer wants us spiritually blind! He has restored in this hour, our sight! Shift and see things from a new perspective, from the point of view of the Kingdom.

Ephesians 2:6 says, "He hath raised us up and seated us in the Heavenly Places in Christ Jesus". Restoration means that we can accept our position as ambassadors on the Earth. As we accept our rightful position, our view changes. See yourself and the world around you from an aerial view. This includes your enemies. GOD is telling us to receive thy sight! Receive upon you the ability to see into the supernatural. Receive your ability to discern at a higher rate of efficacy to wage war on the enemy.

See from a New Paradigm!

A paradigm is an example or pattern in science. It is a theoretical framework. It is the way we think. God is calling for us to shift into the supernatural patterns of the Kingdom. He is calling us to change the way we think so that we think supernaturally. In the Kingdom of God, the supernatural is our normal. We will be able to see further and deeper into the realms of the supernatural as we allow God to change our paradigm. He is endowing us to see and function from a new perspective.

How we think is directly correlated with how we perceive or interpret vision. Our pattern is found in the scriptures. The supernatural is manifested when we follow the patterns (paradigms) found in scripture. A Biblical example of what happens when we see from God's view is found in the example of Elisha and his servant.

II Kings 6:15-17 reads, "When the servant of the man of God got up early the next morning and went outside, there were troops, horses, and chariots everywhere. 'Oh, sir, what will we do now?' the young man cried to Elisha. 'Don't be afraid!' Elisha told him. 'For there are more on our side than on theirs!' Then Elisha prayed, 'O LORD, open his eyes and let him see!' The LORD opened the young man's eyes, and when he looked up, he saw that the hillside around Elisha was filled with horses and chariots of fire".

Elisha told his servant to see or to look again! To do something again means that it has to be done over. When the servant looked again, he was able to see into the spirit. He was able to see beyond the limits of the natural eye. God is increasing our sight so that we may see beyond the natural eye and even see ourselves how HE sees us!

Father says to His people:

Take the limits off of your sight! It is when you see it that you are able to seize it. You must be able to see in order to seize. See your destiny and grab hold of it. See your purpose and grab hold of it. Take it and run. For behold I am doing a new thing in you, for you, and around you. Can you see it? GRAB IT AND RUN!

When Elisha prayed, it changed his servant's eyesight and his perspective. In order to see differently, we must be able to think differently. *"For as a man thinks so is he" (Proverbs 23:7).*

See and Believe!

Another key to living in the supernatural is the ability to see and believe God for miracles. *Numbers 11:23-25 says, "And the Lord said unto Moses, Is the Lord's hand waxed short? Thou shalt see now whether my word shall come to pass or not."* God wants us to see His Word come to pass. He is manifesting the fruit of His promises to us NOW! He is restoring the fruit of the promise to us NOW! As we progress into the lifestyle of open Heaven living, we will begin to see instant results that prove that God is God. God wants to prove Himself through you! He is already proving Himself through us! Each time that we serve and love, we bring His Word to pass. Each time that we speak, dance, and decree the Word, God will bring it to pass.

Mark 9:23 says, "'What do you mean, if I can?' Jesus asked. Anything is possible if a person believes" (NLT). In context, a man was seeking a miracle for his son's condition. The Greek word for believe is pisteuo and means to think to be true, to be persuaded, or to place confidence in. Christ's response expressed that there is no such thing as "if" in God. All things are "yes" and "amen." All things can happen in Christ when we believe we are able to see manifestations. We have to believe for the now. Kingdom believers will see more miracles when we expand in our ability to believe for the supernatural.

The difference between healing and miracles is that healing can be progressive, and miracles are instantaneous. God can and is able to do both. *Matthew 9:29 says, "Then he touched their eyes and said, 'According to your faith let it be done to you'"* (NLT). We are to expect miracles. God is calling for us to increase in expectation of His power. Biblically, people went to where Jesus was because they were in expectation to receive something from Him. They expected miracles. The same is true of the Apostles as studied in the Book of Acts. We are to live the present-day Acts. Father is revealing that people will come to us (not just at church) in expectation to receive something from Him. Therefore, we must also expect that He will give something through us to His people.

Romans 8:19 says, "For the creation waits in eager expectation for the children of God to be revealed" (NLT). The Earth is waiting for us to manifest. Someone is believing and waiting on a miracle. Someone needs to be free from emotional bondage. Someone needs a miracle so that they are healed from cancer. Someone even needs financial miracles. Father has sent us to not only be beautiful dancers but to be dancing miracles. By moving on what we believe, we can activate someone else's faith, causing them to believe. Believing is what allows us to step into miracles. Miracles cause a reproduction of more believers.

Ephesians 3:20 says, "Now to Him who is able to do immeasurably more than all we ask or think or imagine, according to His power that is at work in us". God's power is at work in us. All we have to do is see and believe! There are no limits to what God can do. When we see and believe God now, miracles will happen. All things—healing, wholeness, deliverance, signs, and wonders—are available to us NOW! Doubt is not an option in the supernatural.

James 1:6 says, "But when you ask, you must believe and not doubt, because the one who doubts is like a wave of the sea, blown and tossed by the wind. That person should not expect to receive anything from the Lord". God gives us permission to ask for miracles! Doubt is one of the enemies of miracles. It causes us to be limited in faith when God is truth, and His truth is unlimited. Doubt halts the flow of the river of the supernatural by causing our spirits to be out of alignment with the flow of the Holy Spirit. We must be aligned with the Holy Spirit so that He may flow freely through us. Essentially, this means that we must lay down our life so that the Holy Spirit lives freely through us. Doubt happens when we live a life of the flesh and not of the Spirit.

Believing for miracles begins with us. *John 10:38 says, "But if I do his work, believe in the evidence of the miraculous works I have done, even if you don't believe me. Then you will know and understand that the Father is in me, and I am in the Father"* (NLT). Jesus shared the Kingdom by giving miracles and caused many to believe in the Father. Miracles are the way that we encourage others to believe. This is why we must believe God for miracles first. As we carry out the supernatural as sent ambassadors, we reveal who God is, and

His love towards His people. If we avail ourselves (all that we are and all that we do), the miraculous happens. The result of this is Kingdom expansion.

Be encouraged to see and believe in new ways. God has already put it inside of us. What was once tossed aside and counted out is available NOW! See again, and believe again!

Supernatural Concepts Applied

1. *What are three things that you are believing God for?*

2. *What steps can you take now to prepare yourself to see the manifestation of those three things?*

3. *How do you plan to serve as an ambassador for Christ through your dance?*

Chapter Six

DANCING BEYOND THE
EIGHT COUNTS

We are oftentimes taught to "go in," which is in alignment with the teaching of the Tabernacle of Moses. We have learned how to reach the holiest of all. God is saying, "Don't stop there! Ascend!" God is calling for us to ascend into Heaven and bring down manifestations of God's tangible presence. We were created to praise, worship, and to be supernatural. God is calling for us to shift in paradigms so that our dance is transformed from being a dance to being a gateway—a portal to the supernatural.

Mark 16:15-18 says: And then he told them, "Go into all the world and preach the Good News to everyone. Anyone who believes and is baptized will be saved. But anyone who refuses to believe will be condemned. These miraculous signs will accompany those who believe: They will cast out demons in my name, and they will speak in new languages. They will be able to handle snakes with safety, and if they drink anything poisonous, it won't hurt them. They will be able to place their hands on the sick, and they will be healed." (NLT)

This is our mandate in the Kingdom—to believe in miracles and to share the gospel of the Kingdom not only in word, but in power. The purpose of why we dance has expanded. We worship God in dance to acknowledge who He is. We praise God in dance to acknowledge His mighty works. We also dance to demonstrate God's supernatural power on the Earth. All of these are how we are used by God to expand God's Kingdom (His government and His rulership) on the Earth as sent ambassadors. In *I Corinthians 2:4, Paul the Apostle says, "And my speech and my preaching was not with enticing words of man's wisdom, but in demonstration of the Spirit and of power"* (NLT).

Every believer is called to operate in miracles, signs, and wonders. We are being sent to bring healing, deliverance, miracles, as well as all manifestations of Heaven through our dance. We are not just dancers. Our ministry surpasses beyond a series of eight counts and beautiful technique. Dance ministers must walk in the divine revelation sent by God with a greater purpose. Dance is the avenue by which we are sent into various environments or spheres to create change.

Dancing in the supernatural realm begins with our faith to believe that God is still in the miracle-working business. First, we must dance by faith. Additionally, we must be totally surrendered to the anointing or divine grace of God. It is in the anointing that God dances through us. When we reach this place of total yielding then we are ready to cross over beyond the eight counts into the glory realm—the realm of the supernatural. In this realm lies the power to heal, cast our devils, prophesy, and manifest God's presence according to how the Holy Spirit chooses.

Dances of the supernatural is a form of Kingdom advancement that functions and dwells beyond the eight counts. This is that place beyond the dance called glory. God is calling us deeper. He wants us to go to higher dimensions in Him. In the Old Testament, we learned about the outer court, holy place, and holies of holies (Exodus Chapters 26 and 27). In the New Testament, Jesus Himself came as the final tabernacle (Hebrews 9:11, source). The veil that once separated us from God was torn when Christ died for us. He then sent us His precious Holy Spirit to dwell in us and with us. As we look at dances of the supernatural, we have to explore what happens beyond the veil. Since the veil was done away with and the power source put inside of us—what's next? What do we do with this freedom in grace? How can the unveiled life where Heaven touches Earth be transformed into and through dance? God has revealed a concept called dances of the supernatural. Through this paradigm, dance is no longer just a series of eight counts. It is ministry.

There are three elements: faith, anointing, and glory. These dimensions can also be referred to as levels, or elements, in dances of the supernatural. God uses these elements as a means to take us higher and deeper into His presence. It is God's desire for us to penetrate through each of these levels; each dimension is progressive and takes us deeper into God's presence causing Him to manifest Himself through us.

First Dimension and Element:
Becoming an Atmosphere and Ministering by Faith

The definition of faith is risk. We have to take risks and trust the Holy Spirit for healing, deliverance, miracles, etc. We are to take the risks by faith and yield to what the Holy Spirit tells us to do. This means that the minister must be ok if the Holy Spirit shifts the choreography. Make sure that it's Him so that the shift is done with efficacy. Again, one cannot operate in the supernatural without faith. Faith is defined as a complete confidence in someone or something, a strong belief in God and His Doctrine based on spiritual apprehension or persuasion rather than proof. *Hebrews 10:38 says, "But my righteous one shall live by faith, and if he shrinks back, my soul has no pleasure in him."* We are never to shrink back from being our supernatural selves.

An atmosphere is defined as an envelope of gases surrounding a planet, or the pervading mood or tone of a place, situation; character. Mankind was God's only creation that He breathed life into. We also were made in the image and likeness of God (Genesis 1:27, Gen 2:7). This denotes that we are made to emulate the character of God. We are an atmosphere, and because of this revelation, we create an environment for what God wants to do in the Earthly realm. Practices that are important to being an atmosphere for God's supernatural use, include, but are not limited to:

- Audible prayer and prayer through movement(Jude 1:20), building ourselves up on holy faith and by prayer in the Holy Ghost (James 5:16), fervent prayer

- Praise (Psalms 100, Psalms 150, Revelations 19:4-6)

- United sound (Romans 15:6)

- Consistent intimate worship

*Please note that this is most important to build in private with an audience of one not only during a worship celebration.

**Second Dimension and Element:
Ministering Under the Anointing –
DON'T THINK! YIELD!**

Once we have completely let go of ourselves and have gone into a yielded state of dance. The Holy Spirit is in complete control of the dance minister's body. When reaching this state in dance, most ministers of dance stop here. Once the music is over, stay there because there may be more that God wants to do. We must train our ear to hear the Holy Spirit and train our eyes to look in the spirit. He will give instructions even during our worship and choreography. It is important that we do not box God in or out. It is important that we do not try to reason away the supernatural; rather we are to yield to the leading of the Holy Spirit. We are to see and hear what the Lord is revealing and heed to the instructions given. Good meditation scriptures for this concept are:

- Isaiah 55:3,6 - Incline your ear to hear.

- Revelations 3:22 - He who has an ear let him hear what the Spirit says.

- John - 10:27 My sheep know my voice and listen.

Anointing means to smear or rub with oil, or a divine enablement. Every believer has an anointing and is empowered by God to serve as a supernatural agent. The anointing comes from and is the Holy Spirit. Isaiah 61:1-3 says:

The Spirit of the Sovereign LORD is upon me, for the LORD has anointed me to bring good news to the poor. He has sent me to comfort the brokenhearted and to proclaim that captives will be released and prisoners will be freed.2 He has sent me to tell those who mourn that the time of the LORD's favor has come, and with it, the day of God's anger against their enemies. To all who mourn in Israel, he will give a crown of beauty for ashes, a joyous blessing instead of mourning, festive praise instead of despair. In their righteousness, they will be like great oaks that the LORD has planted for his own glory. (NLT)

This is the overall purpose of Christ's ascension—to be living witnesses of His power. We are to go to every nation to share the gospel and to bring the light of God to all corners of the Earth. Every Believer, at the time of salvation receives the indwelling of the Holy Spirit. This means He takes residence inside of us at the time of salvation. Every believer also was given the provision to be activated in the infilling of the Holy Spirit through the baptism of the Holy Spirit. God gave us the baptism of the Holy Spirit, not only for the purposes of speaking in tongues but so that we may operate in the power of Christ on the Earth.

Acts 1:8 says, "But you will receive power when the Holy Spirit comes upon you. And you will be my witnesses, telling people about me everywhere--in Jerusalem, throughout Judea, in Samaria, and to the ends of the earth". The word power in this passage comes from the Greek word dynamis and means to have the strength, ability, and power to perform miracles. We are all endowed with power through the anointing of the Holy Ghost to minister miracles and all things supernatural.

There is a second type of power that God has given us in Christ, who is our authority. Christ at the time of His death, burial, resurrection, and ascension provided us with authority over Satan, death, and the power of sin. *Matthew 10:1 says, "And when he had called unto him his twelve disciples, he gave them power against unclean spirits, to cast them out, and to heal all manner of sickness and all manner of disease"* (NLT) The word power in this passage comes from the Greek word exousia and means authority, right, or liberty, a thing subject to authority or rule. The kingdom of darkness is subject to the rule of the Kingdom of Heaven. In Christ we have authority to cast out devils, heal the sick, and raise the dead. Another definition of exousia power is to have rule over a jurisdiction. As Kingdom citizens, the Earth is our jurisdiction where we manage domestic affairs by legislating Heaven on Earth. The Earth is the sphere or domain that God has given us. His has given us delegated authority and rulership over it.

It is important to note that one cannot operate in ability only. We must have both power and authority. This means we cannot we cannot effectively operate in authority without first submitting to the authority of the Lord. This is vital to function in the supernatural power of God (see Acts 19:11-20).

To summarize:
dynamis = ability and exousia = authority

Dances of the Supernatural Defy Laws of Worldly Dance:

God nor His power is confined to time, space, or matter. Therefore, He does everything independently of worldly principles. For example, He can cause blind eyes to see or cause a person to do something they could not do before (such as walk or dance). These are types of miracles that God wants to manifest on the Earth. He has designed dance to be an avenue for these types of manifestations. In this regard, dances of the supernatural are independent of any limits that the world may have set for them— we are not confined to the stage nor to an eight count. With this in mind, dance ministers must:

• Know the difference between performance and ministry,

• Know who we are as servants, and

• Understand that our identity and authority in Christ causes us to function in the supernatural.

It is important to mention that when reaching this point in the crossover, knowing the protocol and order of the set ministry that we are sent to is important. We have to make sure that the assignment will allow for the supernatural to manifest. Do everything decently and in order. When ministering at a church or local fellowship, get clearance from the leadership at that house. This can be accomplished in a meeting with the leadership. *Romans 13:1 says, "Every one must submit to governing authorities. For all authority comes from God, and those in positions of authority have been placed there by God"* (NLT). Submission to authority is a facet of unity along with united worship, which also aids in creating an environment that is conducive for the supernatural. Additionally, we do not want our good intentions to be twisted or mistaken for bad motives so we must honor spheres of all authority (*Romans 14:16* NLT).

Third Dimension and Element: The Glory
Going Beyond the Eight Counts
(Miracles, Signs, and Wonders)

The third dimension and element is the supernatural dimension— the Glory realm. In this dimension, the minister has crossed over from being a dancer to a minister of dance (servant of the Lord through dance). The minister has crossed over into the portals of Heaven! This is where we can operate in the same manner as Christ!

Believe me when I say that I am in the Father and the Father is in me; or at least believe on the evidence of the works themselves. Very truly I tell you, whoever believes in me will do the works I have been doing, and they will do even greater things than these, because I am going to the Father. (John 14:11-12)

As Kingdom agents, we are the living evidence that Jesus is Lord! Through prophecy, healing, deliverance, miracles, signs, and wonders, we bring heaven to earth, declaring that God and the resurrection of Jesus is real. This is how we testify to Jesus. We must follow the Biblical patterns of Christ and the Apostles. Salvation was received through the visible demonstrations of God's power. Through our dance, we are able to make the invisible visible so that others will be led to receive Jesus into their hearts.

The supernatural is the place where God will encourage the dance minister to engage his people. This can manifest in a limitless number of ways such as:

- Prophecy

- Laying on of hands

- Simply holding someone as they cry

- Deliverance and healing

- Words of knowledge

- Decreeing God's Word (even without laying on of hands)

- The effective use of Prophetic worship tools (weaponry)

- Partnering with the apostolic and prophetic mantles

In the supernatural dimension, we pour out God's heart and operate in manifestation gifts. The word gift comes from the Greek word charisma and is defined as an unmerited favor, divine grace, virtue, or graces that denote extraordinary powers. These gifts are given to every believer and can rise in us at any time whenever the Lord wills.

I Corinthians 12: 4-13 says: *Now there are varieties of gifts, but the same Spirit. And there are varieties of ministries, and the same Lord. There are varieties of effects, but the same God who works all things in all persons. But to each one is given the manifestation of the Spirit for the common good. For to one is given the word of wisdom through the Spirit, and to another the word of knowledge according to the same Spirit; to another faith by the same Spirit, and to another gifts of healing by the one Spirit, and to another the effecting of miracles, and to another prophecy, and to another the distinguishing of spirits, to another various kinds of tongues, and to another the interpretation of tongues. But one and the same Spirit works all these things, distributing to each one individually just as He wills. For even as the body is one and yet has many members, and all the members of the body, though they are many, are one body, so also is Christ. For by one Spirit we were all baptized into one body, whether Jews or Greeks, whether slaves or free, and we were all made to drink of one Spirit.*

There are nine manifestation gifts by which the Holy Spirit may choose to operate. Each one is available to every believer, but the Holy Spirit can cause us to function in some more frequently than others.

Gift	Description of the Gift	Scripture Reference and Definition
Revelatory Gifts: These are the manifestation gifts God uses to reveal His mind and heart. What God reveals through these gifts cannot be received any other way except by revelation.		
Words of Wisdom	Divine enablement to receive divine insight and strategy for a particular scenario	I Cor 12:8 – Sophia: the act of interpreting and giving advice, discovering the meaning of vision, broad knowledge of diverse matters
Words of Knowledge	Supernatural revelation of information that one did not know before	I Cor 14:6, I Cor 12;8 – Gnosis: general knowledge or understanding
Distinguishing of Spirits	The supernatural ability to distinguish between the truth of the Word and the deceptive doctrines of demons	John 4:1, I Cor 12:10 – Diakrisis: to distinguish, or judge, to separate, or make distinction, to contend
Power Gifts: These are the gifts that God uses to physically do things for others on Earth as it is in Heaven.		
Faith	Supernatural confidence in God's promises, power, and presence	James 2:18 – Pistis: conviction of truth; belief

Gift	Description of the Gift	Scripture Reference and Definition
Healings	Supernatural manifestation of the Spirit of God that miraculously brings healing and deliverance from disease and/or infirmity	Luke 9:11 – Iaomai: to cure to make whole
Miracles	The Supernatural intervention of the power of God that alters the course of nature	Acts 19:11-12 – Dynamis: power for performing miracles
Vocal Gifts: These are the manifestation gifts that God uses to verbally express Himself on the Earth.		
Prophecy	The Supernatural ability to interpret and speak forth (proclaim) the divine will and purposes of God	I Cor 14:3-5 – Propheteuo: to speak forth by divine inspiration, to declare a thing by divine revelation
Diverse Tongues	The Supernatural ability to speak in a language never before learned in order to reach someone who does speak a particular language	I Cor 12:10 – Genos: offspring, family, kindred, miracles Glossa: an organ of speech, the language or dialect used by a particular people distinct from that of other nations
Interpretation of Tongues	The Supernatural ability to speak in a known language the utterance that was spoken in an unknown language	I Cor 12:10 - Hermeneia: interpretation of what has been spoken obscurely by others

These nine gifts are manifested in the glory realm. Again, the glory realm is not dependent on time, space, or matter. *John 2:11 says, "This beginning of miracles did Jesus in Cana of Galilee, and manifested forth his glory; and his disciples believed on him"* (NLT). The Greek word for glory is the word doxa, which refers to God's splendor; it is the most glorious condition or exalted state. Glory is the presence of God. Jesus manifested His glory to encourage the faith of both believers and those who did not yet believe.

II Corinthians 3:18 says, "But we all, with unveiled face, beholding as in a mirror the glory of the Lord, are being transformed into the same image from glory to glory, just as from the Lord, the Spirit" (NLT).

This same glory He put inside of each of us. God gave us the divine ability to live in Heaven and on Earth at the same time. We are meant to carry the glory and function in the glory of God. The Holy Spirit, who lives inside of us, provides for us the ability to live in the glory realm. The Glory is God's presence. God literally put His presence in us through the person of the Holy Spirit. This is why we must get to know the Holy Spirit as our friend. He is the glory of God inside of us, who allows us to be carriers of His presence—glory carriers. The glory element of Dances of the Supernatural reveals that we are to dance with the understanding to reflect his glory in the Earth.

When we enter into the dances of the supernatural, we enter into God's presence, where miracles are released. It is God's desire to restore even creative miracles to the Church. We must be postured to be limitless for this type of ministry to flow freely. In the realm of glory, all things are possible!

Hebrews 2:4 says, "And God confirmed the message by giving signs and wonders and various miracles and gifts of the Holy Spirit wherever He chose" (NLT) God will confirm His presence through miracles, signs, and wonders. He will confirm His presence through us! He will use our dances to activate the gifts of the Spirit so that others will see that He is real.

Ephesians 3:16 says, "I pray that from his glorious, unlimited resources he will empower you with inner strength through His Spirit" (NLT). We must release the dances of the supernatural because they open the door for the limitless possibilities of God to be made known to His people. It is God's will for us to manifest His glory on the Earth. The third dimension of supernatural dance is where the Holy Spirit brings all that we are together for His purpose. Again, nothing can be done apart from the Holy Spirit.

Therefore, dances of the supernatural are birthed from*:

•   Our worship as a lifestyle

- Studying of scriptures (learn to dance the scriptures)

- A consecrated lifestyle of living the scriptures

- Our personal encounters with God (our testimony)

- Remaining united with the body of Christ

*Please Note: This is not to say that we have to seek to be perfect because God's grace is sufficient. Just embrace the grace and draw near to God by continuing to build a close relationship with HIM! As we do this, we are inclined to be led to Him with precision. He will reveal His heart for His people, which will manifest through our dance. He will take us beyond the eight counts!

These are meditation scriptures to build faith for the supernatural:

- John 8:36 - We are free indeed

- II Timothy 2:15 - Study

- Matthew 5:16-17 - Let your light shine

- Galatians 14:6 - Abba Father (relationship)

- Psalms 42:1-2 - As the deer pants for the water (continual deepening of relationship)

Be empowered to release dances of the supernatural! Ascend into the presence and power of God.

Supernatural Concepts Applied

1. *We each have an anointing. What do you believe is your anointing?*

2. *How can you partner your anointing with the anointing of others to encounter the supernatural?*

3. *The manifestation gifts are given freely as the Lord wills. Which of the manifestation gifts do you believe you operate in? How have you used them to serve others?*

Chapter Seven

MOVE ON PURPOSE
AND IN PURPOSE

The time is over for Church as usual. People are in search of a now movement from God. The supernatural is what God uses to win souls to confirm our ministry. *Hebrews 2:4 says, "God also bearing them witness both with signs and wonders, and with divers miracles, and gifts of the Holy Ghost, according to His own will".* Dance is the vehicle through which we are sent. Following the pattern of the scriptures reveals that our dances can longer be just be a series of eight counts. They must be dances that activate movement from heaven to earth. The supernatural is what God gave us to accompany us as we are serving through dance. There are many miracles waiting to be manifested and many souls waiting to encounter the true love of Christ.

The supernatural manifests through the senses. This chapter is designed to help worshipers explore how the Lord moves in the supernatural and what it could look like. In order to understand that the Lord will speak in various ways, we have to settle on the fact that God is always moving with us and constantly moving on our behalf when we minister. It is up to us to see and hear what the Lord is saying in the spirit then connect with Him to implement it in the Earth. *Mark 16:20 states, "And they went forth, and preached every where, the Lord working with them, and confirming the word with signs following".*

In context, this occurred after Jesus' ascension, and after Jesus gave the Apostles, along with others who were present, what we have come to know as the Great Commission. For the new covenant worshiper, we are sent to serve and carry out the Great Commission, through dance, is knowing that everywhere we are sent we have the power to manifest the presence of God. There must be intentionality to implement this mandate—to preach the gospel of the Kingdom as we serve through dance. This is more than ministering a series of eight counts with a beautiful garment on.

There are several ways that God will speak to us, even through our dance. The Lord is able to speak to us through natural senses. This only works as we allow our natural senses to be yielded to the sense of the spirit. In other words, if we are spiritually sensitive, we will be able to feel what God feels and to see what He sees.

II Timothy 2:21 instructs us, *"If you keep yourself pure, you will be a special utensil for honorable use. Your life will be clean, and you will ready for the Master to use you for every good work".* Being yielded to the spirit comes with a readiness to be used by God at any given time. This also denotes that the supernatural is a lifestyle that involves purity. There is grace for our mistakes; however, it is not ok to live in blatant rebellion towards God.

Moving on purpose and in purpose means that we function as the Father functions from a heart of love. Love must be the single motivator in everything that we do, especially when serving in the supernatural. Jesus sets thee example for this. *Matthew 9:36 says, "But when he saw the multitudes, he was moved with compassion on them, because they fainted and were scattered abroad, as sheep having no shepherd".*

The word compassion in this passage means to be moved in the bowels, which is the seat of love and pity *(G4697)*. The word compassion is also synonymous with the word love. Love is what moves our triune God and love is also what should move us from just looking to serving. Jesus didn't just look at people and judge them; he moved to help them. We find a principle here for the new covenant worshiper: we are use our movement to help others through a heart of compassion. Without love as our motivator, we have and are doing nothing (*I Corinthians 13*).

Father is saying, that as you're reading this, you will experience a heart-breaking encounter with the Lord. Once you have this encounter, you will be touched and moved by what touches and moves God. As you enter into this revelation, the trajectory of your approach to the worship arts will take a dramatic shift. You will now have a heightened awareness of the supernatural impact that God wants for His people at any given time and in any given place. You have now entered into your sent place.

Ways that the Lord Manifests

The Lord chooses to manifest the gifts according to His will. At times, He communicates the gifts to us through our senses. Included are examples of how the Lord reveals Himself and His purposes through the senses. Please note that these are only examples to help raise awareness of when the Lord may be communicating with us. The Holy Spirit is and can speak in various ways.

The Eyes to see

Matthew 13:15,16 says, "For this people's heart has become calloused they hardly hear with their ears, and they have closed their eyes. Otherwise they might see with their eyes, hear with their ears, understand with their heart and turn, and I would heal them. But blessed are your eyes because they see, and your ears because they hear."

This scripture refers to the importance of believing. Our eyes, hearts, and ears have to be postured to be open to the supernatural moves of God. We may receive and give the blessings that the Lord is releasing.

This concept also has to deal with what we see and how we see. We must be able to see how the Lord sees through faith and compassion. Conversely, seeing in the supernatural allows us to operate in the revelatory gifts of perception. For example, in God we are able to discern the presence of both angels and demons. When God allows us to see this way, we must ask the Holy Spirit what He would like for us to do.

God deals with the eyes by:

- Causing something to be brighter

- Allowing us to see words

- Snapshot visions

- Rapid eye movement while awake (This typically happens during a vision or visitation)

The Ears to Hear

Mark 4:24 says, "And he said to them, 'Pay attention to what you hear: with the measure you use, it will be measured to you, and still more will be added to you'" (NLT).

We are to pay attention to what we hear in the natural and the Spirit. The instruction given in the latter part of the verse serves as a key to function in the supernatural; we are to use what we hear so that more may be heard. We are not only to hear what the Lord says, but we are also given the ability to ask Him what to do with what we have heard.

God can speak to us through His still small voice. In terms of revelations, we can hear the following:

- Words or phrases

- A whisper

- Unction in word form from the Holy Spirit

- Instructions

Healing Hands

Acts 4:30 says, "Stretch out your hand with healing power; may miraculous signs and wonders be done through the name of your holy servant Jesus" (NLT).

The Apostles prayed that the Lord would stretch forth His hand to prove the preached word. This reveals that the Lord doesn't need us to always lay hands on people; however, there are times when the Lord wants to use our hands to do the work of Heaven through the laying on of hands.

We see Jesus modeling this example for us: *"While the sun was setting, all those who had any who were sick with various diseases brought them to Him; and laying His hands on each one of them, He was healing them" (Luke 4:40).* There are various ways that the Lord may choose to heal. He lived out this example for us so that we may live out what He modeled.

Signs of healing hands include but are not limited to:

• Feeling heat on the hands

• Tingling of the hands

• Shaking of the hands

A Genuine Heart to Feel

Matthew 9:36 says, "But when he saw the multitudes, he was moved with compassion on them, because they fainted, and were scattered abroad, as sheep having no shepherd" (NLT).

• The word compassion is described as having pity. Jesus was moved in pity towards those he saw who were hurting. He did not judge them. He healed them.

• The Spirit of the Lord will allow us to feel or have a sense of good and bad. At times, we may even feel physical pain that is not ours. This is a way of communication that the Lord uses to allow us to sense when someone around us may be in need of prayer.

Impressions Upon the Mind

Matthew 9:4 says, "Jesus knew what they were thinking, so he asked them, 'Why do you have such evil thoughts in your hearts?'" (NLT).

In context, this is an example of a word of knowledge or a supernatural revelation of information that was previously unknown. Jesus knew what the Scribes were thinking, and he responded. The Father speaks supernaturally to us by giving us a spontaneous thought. This is an impression on the mind to do something and leads to a particular response.

Words Spoken out the Mouth

Then Peter said, "Silver or gold I do not have, but what I do have I give you. In the name of Jesus Christ of Nazareth, walk." Taking him by the right hand, he helped him up, and instantly the man's feet and ankles became strong. He jumped to his feet and began to walk. Then he went with them into the temple courts, walking and jumping, and praising God..." (Acts 3: 6-8, NLT)

In this passage, Peter spoke to the man at the gate and gave him what He needed to change his condition. The Lord will give us just what to say to cause a situation to change. The Lord chose to speak to the man through Peter to heal him. God intends to speak to us in a similar manner according to the following ways:

- Prophetic utterances (forth-telling or foretelling)

- Decrees and declarations

- Prayer

- Tongues and interpretation

- Speaking directly by changing our words over

Again, these examples are inexhaustible. It is important to pay attention to how the Lord is speaking and to move on what He says. Embrace this as a lifestyle that results in cultivating a deep friendship with the triune God.

Supernatural Concepts Applied

1. *What are some ways that the dance can be used in a more purposeful way?*

2. *Of the various ways that the Lord communicates the supernatural to us, which have you experienced most frequently?*

3. *How can you deepen your awareness so that you are able to further receive communication from God?*

Chapter Eight
UNITED WE WORSHIP

Understanding the three-dimensional elements of the supernatural is important individually because when we join these three, God causes a powerful manifestation of His glory in Kingdom gatherings. Unity in worship is God's way of strategically infiltrating His power from Heaven onto the Earth. United worship activates the supernatural, and as believers, the supernatural is normal.

The various forms of worship mentioned in the Bible mirror the activity in Heaven. Worship can be demonstrated in various forms. God gives us many options to choose from to worship and praise Him. No matter how we worship and praise Him, it comes together as a pleasing sight to the Lord. Throughout the scriptures, we see examples of how the assembling of believers invokes the supernatural power of God.

When the day of Pentecost came, they were all together in one place. Suddenly a sound like the blowing of a violent wind came from heaven and filled the whole house where they were sitting. They saw what seemed to be tongues of fire that separated and came to rest on each of them. All of them were filled with the Holy Spirit and began to speak in other tongues as the Spirit enabled them. (Acts 2:1-4, NLT)

In this passage, there was a gathering of believers worshiping on one accord, resulting in what we now know as the Pentecost. This supernatural miracle still lives with us today as the baptism and infilling of the Holy Spirit. It is this infilling that enables us to live in the supernatural. When we gather together and join faith and anointings, the environment for the glory of God to be revealed is created.

God is increasing these glory encounters through the mandate of unity. The scriptures tell is that we have a responsibility to equip and unite the body (*Ephesians 4:11-13*, NLT). Not only are we to learn about the supernatural, but we are to be intentional about coming together so that the supernatural power of God can be experienced by believers and non-believers. It is no longer enough to come together to have services as usual. Worship dancers can no longer minister dances as usual. There is a mandate from Heaven for us to pursue unity and to seek to encounter the tangible presence of God so that the Kingdom of Heaven is made visible.

The scriptures paint a picture of what the sights of united worship is to look like is Psalm 150:

Praise ye the Lord. Praise God in his sanctuary: praise him in the firmament of his power. Praise him for his mighty acts: praise him according to his excellent greatness. Praise him with the sound of the trumpet: praise him with the psaltery and harp. Praise him with the timbrel and dance: praise him with stringed instruments and organs. Praise him up on the loud cymbal: praise him upon the high sounding cymbals. Let everything that hath breath praise the Lord. Praise ye the Lord. (NLT)

Here, we have an outline of what worship is supposed to look like. Psalm 150 uses song, music, dance, and the scripture itself as poetry. It doesn't say to take turns, but the Word tells us to praise. We are to use every avenue/gift available to worship God. The verb praise used throughout Psalm 150 means to be clear (of sound, or color), to shine, to boast, to be clamorously foolish, or to celebrate *(Strong's H1984)*. This means that our worship is to be intense. To celebrate God requires movement paired with another tool of worship. Sure one person can be clamorously foolish but how much more effective can a whole group of people make his name great through worshiping God in multiple ways at one time?

The first two verses tell us where and why we praise him. The last four verses tells us how to praise God. The word firmament comes from the Hebrew word raqiya and means the expanse or the visible arch of the sky *(Strong's H549)*. Its deeper meaning comes from the word raqa, which means to pound the earth as a sign of passion, to overlay with thin sheets of metal, to beat to make broad, to stamp, or to stretch *(Strong's H7554)*. We are to praise and worship him all over Earth—even the Earth was made as an instrument of praise. The Earth essentially was made to be a drum before the Lord. A drum cannot be played without the movement of the hands and feet. The deeper definition of the firmament shows us that the hands and feet can be used to partner with the Earth as a drum as we stomp or strike the ground with the hands or heel as in tap dancing, for example. The Earth, along with the movement of the body, then becomes an instrument before God and is partnered together with dancing to bring Him glory.

Psalms 150 reveals to us the foundation of partnerships in worship. It reveals that praise is to include sound with instruments, the voice with singing, and movement with dance. This reveals that each part is equally important because different combinations produce different results in worship. These results are manifestations of God's power that are produced when we are united in worship.

God's Power Revealed in Unity

And seven priests shall bear before the ark seven trumpets of rams' horns: and the seventh day ye shall compass the city seven times, and the priests shall blow with the trumpets. And it shall come to pass, that when they make a long blast with the rams' horn, and when ye hear the sound of the trumpet, all the people shall shout with a great shout: and the wall of the city shall fall down flat, and the people shall ascend every man straight before them. (Joshua 6:4, 5)

During the assignment that was given to Joshua at Jericho, the Lord chose to use movement, sound, and instruments to conquer Jericho. This combination, in this instance, was a war strategy that would cause the Israelites to triumph over Jericho.

The word compass in this passage means to turn about, around, aside, or back towards, to encircle *(Strong's H5437)*. It is associated in root with the following Hebrew verb stems:

1. Qal - to turn about, to change

2. Niphal - to turn oneself

3. Piel - to turn about

4. Poel - to encompass, to assemble around, to envelop

5. Hiphil - to turn, to cause to turn, to reverse

6. Hophal - to be turned, to be surrounded

(Strong's Lexicon, blueletterbible.com)

The importance of how the term was used is important for this scripture because it denotes that when something is surrounded—especially by the presence of God—something will definitely happen as a result of His presence.

Until it was time to sound the shofars, the Israelites passed around the city seven times in silence. Silence is an element of worship that can be partnered with other forms of worship. By having the Israelites march around the wall sent a silent message, thus causing the act to be a declaration in the spirit realm that the wall was coming down. *Habakkuk 2:20 says, "But the Lord is in His holy temple; let all the earth keep silence before him"* (ESV). Silence is a sign of humility and worship in the presence of God. In this instance, the Israelites kept silent in worship until the appointed time, then they released a sound, and God moved on their behalf.

As the priests marched around the walls, they enveloped the city of Jericho with God's presence, causing the walls of Jericho to weaken. After the processional was completed seven times, He told the priests to sound the trumpets, which comes from the

Hebrew word showphar and a horn, or ram's horn. John J. Parson writes in his article, "Significance of the Shofar the Shout of God's Victory," "The shofar (ram's horn) is often used as an instrument of spiritual warfare… Apart from these purposes the shofar was also used sound alarms for the camp of Israel. The shofar was also used when Joshua waged war against Jericho and during other military campaigns. Indeed, when Israel engaged the enemy in battle, the priests and Levites would first prepare the way by sounding the shofar" *(hebrewforchristians.com)*. The shofar combined with movement and sound in this passage prepared the way for the Israelites and also made the Canaanites aware that the Israelites were ready for battle and that the Lord was with them.

Next, the Israelites released a shout. The word shout is translated to the Hebrew word ruwa and means to mar by breaking, to split the ears with sound, to shout an alarm or joy, to destroy, to make a joyful noise, to cry out in distress *(Strong's H7321)*. Combined with the processional and the trumpets, the released sound not only split the ears but caused a breaking down of the walls of Jericho. It was when the sound the instruments and the movement came together that the walls came down.

Bringing all the forms of worship together in unity invites God's glory to fill not only the room but the hearts of men. *II Chronicles 5:13,14 says, "It even came to pass, as the trumpeters and singers were as one sound to be heard in praising and thanking the Lord; and when they lift up their voice with the trumpets and cymbals and instruments of musick and praised the Lord saying, For he is good for his good, for his mercy endureth forever: that then the house was filled with a cloud, even the house of the Lord. So that the priests could not stand to minister by reason of the cloud, even the house of the Lord."* This passage of scripture contains song, music, and dance.

Each aspect mentioned in this passage represents a piece to the puzzle of worship. The trumpeter refers to the players on clarion, or to sound with a clarion or quavering note (Strong's H2690 and H2689). The trumpet is a wind instrument and is the highest register of the brass family. This means that the trumpets or wind instruments carry a penetrating sound that God loves to hear in worship. Music in this passage is a lyric or song, a religious song, or a song of Levitical choirs *(Strong's H7892)*. It comes from the Hebrew word that means strolling minstrels *(Strong's H7891)*. Praise is found again in this passage and has the same instruction to make God's name BIG through our reckless praise. Collectively, these forms of worship came together as one and captured the heart of God, causing Him to fill the room. The ministers could no longer minister because their hearts were on one accord with one another and with God. God honors and responds to unity!

I Chronicles 16:27 says, *"Honor and majesty are found in His presence; strength and joy are found in His sanctuary"* (AMP). Worshiping on one accord identifies us as God's people.

Jesus prays in *John 17:22,23 and says, "And the glory which thou gavest me I have given them: that they may be one, even as we are one. I in them and thou in me, that they may be made perfect in one; and that the world may know that thou hast sent me, and hast loved them, as thou loved me".*

Through united worship, we are activating the on-going ministry of Christ and reflecting the power of our triune God. Jesus wants us to be one—that is to live and operate as one. "The present subjunctive used here designates on-going action: "continually be one", a oneness based on their common relationship to the Father and to the Son" *(Life in the Spirit Study Bible, 2003)*. It is God's will for us to come together with all of our various gifts as one movement, one voice, and one sound to produce Kingdom worship.

All of the various art forms were meant to come together as one. *Psalm 24:1 says, "The earth is the Lord's and the fullness thereof; the world, and they that dwell therein".* Everything that was made was made by the Lord and for Him. As the Creator of worship, He has designed various forms of worship into what we generally understand to be the arts. The arts were made to glorify God. The separation of the arts from worship most likely had an association with the fall of Lucifer from Heaven.

Thou hast been in Eden the garden of God; every precious stone was thy covering, the sardius, topaz, and the diamond, the beryl, the onyx and the jasper, the sapphire the emerald, and the carbuncle, and gold: the workmanship of thy tabrets and of thy pipes was prepared in thee in the day that thou wast created... Thou wast perfect in all thy ways from the day that thou was created, till iniquity was found in thee... Thou hast defiled sanctuaries by the multitude of thine iniquities, by the iniquity of thy traffick; therefore will I bring forth a fire from the midst of thee, it shall devour thee, and I will bring thee to ashes upon the earth in the sight of all them that behold thee. (Ezekiel 28:13, 15, 18)

Lucifer, before he was kicked out of Heaven, was made to worship God. The tabrets mentioned in this passage translate from the Hebrew word toph, meaning timbrel or tambourine *(Strong's H8596)*. It comes from the word taphaph, meaning to play or sound the timbrel to beat upon, drum. Lucifer was an angel of percussion.

Percussion instruments are used to create what is commonly referred to as the melody and harmony of music. The melody is the heartbeat of a musical piece. As an angel of worship, Lucifer had the ability to connect with the heartbeat of God. In his fallen state, he seeks to pervert sound and give a false heartbeat. This is why the mountain of arts and entertainment must be infiltrated by worshipers. The arts, in all its forms, were originally made for worship. Therefore, it is important to protect the anointing and presence of God because Satan seeks to produce a false anointing in the supernatural.

Dancing and Musical Instruments

Revelation 5:8 says, "And when he had taken the book, the four beasts and four and twenty elders fell down before the Lamb, having every one of them, harps and golden vials full of odours, which are the prayers of the people".

In this passage, we see the combination of movement, instruments, and prayer. The term fell in this passage is the Greek word pipto and means to fall down *(Strong's 4098)*. The four beasts fell down in worship. The harp is a stringed instrument and is also referred to in the Bible as a lyre. "In the context of Christianity, heaven is sometimes symbolically depicted as populated by angels playing harps, giving the instruments association of the sacred and heavenly" *(Wikipedia.com)*.

An example of the harp partnered with worship and intercession is found in *I Samuel 16:23: "And it came to pass when the evil spirit from God was upon Saul, that David took a harp, and played with his hand: so Saul was refreshed, and was well, and the evil spirit departed from him"*. Prayer is how we communicate with God. The elements of worship found in Revelations 5:8 come together creating and avenue for intercession.

Biblical worship must originate from the Spirit of God and must seek to please God. *Amos 5:21 and 23 says, "I hate, I despise your feast days, and I will not smell in your solemn assemblies... Take thou away from me the noise of thy songs; for I will not hear the noise of thy viols"*. The word feast in this passage is the Hebrew word chag, or a festival or a feast *(Strong's H2282)*.

It is important to the context of this scripture to note that the Hebrew word nebel comes from the Hebrew word nabel, which means to be senseless, foolish, to wither and fall, fade. This passage shows us the combination of dance, song, and instruments in Biblical forms of worship and how they are connected to the lifestyle of the dancer, singer, or musician. Therefore, our worship being used must come from a pure place. Worship is not to be treated as a ritual but as a personal never-ending encounter with God.

Dancing and Spoken Language
(Prayer, Prophecy, Poetry)

Dance combined with poetry, prayer, or prophecy activates the spirit. By joining these forms of worship together, we not only add to worship services but also the make the voice of God visual. *Ephesians 5:19 says, "Speaking to yourselves in psalms, hymns, and spiritual songs, and making melody in your heart to the Lord".* The word melody is a Greek word that means to pluck off, to cause to vibrate, to play a stringed instrument, to sing to the music of a harp *(Strong's G5567).* The heart is an instrument to God, and it is pleasing to God to allow melody of God to partner with song. Psalms, in this passage, refers to singing Old Testament psalms. Psalms is the book of poetry. Hymns are songs used for adoration, prayer, and praise that typically address a deity or prominent figure *(Wikipedia. com).* Spiritual songs are spontaneous songs that are unpremeditated. Prophetic songs are an example of this. *Ephesians 5:19* reveals the importance of the combination of instruments, prayer, poetry, and song. This combination of worship leads to refreshment, renewal, and revival when used together in worship.

Colossians 3:16 tells us, "Let the word of Christ dwell in you richly in all wisdom; teaching and admonishing one another psalms hymns and spiritual songs, singing with grace in your hearts to the Lord".

When this scripture says the "Word," it is translated from the Greek word logos, and is the uttered word that someone has said, the sayings of Christ, a decree, mandate, or order, moral precepts given by God, Old Testament prophecy, reckoning, the act of speaking, anything reported in speech, or a style of speech. *(Strong's G3056).* This passage combines speaking (scriptures), songs, and poetry as worship that is intended to teach and cultivate growth in the believer.

Dance can be added to these forms of worship through interpretation of the Psalm, hymn, or spiritual song. *I Samuel 2:1 says, "And Hannah prayed, and said my heart rejoiceth in the*

Lord, mine horn is exalted in the Lord: my mouth is enlarged over mine enemies; because I rejoice in thy salvation". Prayer is translated to the Hebrew word palal and means to intervene, to impose, to meditate, to intercede, to pray *(Strong's H6419)*. Hannah prayed to God for her son, and when He came, she praised Him again out of a heart of thanksgiving. The word rejoiceth in this passage translates from the Hebrew word alats and means to jump for joy, exult, to be joyful, triumph *(Strong's H5970)*. Hannah danced before the Lord because of her received blessing. The word horn in this passage is the Hebrew word qeren meaning a horn, strength, flask (container for oil), musical instrument, rays of light *(Strong's H7161)*. Hannah's prophetic song contained the elements of song, dance, prayer, and instruments. Hannah's prophetic song means that she was worshiping God ahead of time for what was to come. The elements of worship that Hannah used work together for the result of prophetic worship.

We see these elements of worship in *Luke 1: 44-47*. It reads, *"For lo, as soon as the voice of thy salutation sounded in my ears, the babe leaped in my womb for joy, and blessed is she that believed: for there shall be a performance of those things which were told her from the Lord. And Mary said, My soul doth magnify the Lord and my spirit hath rejoiced in god my Saviour".*

The word leaped in this passage comes from the Greek word skirtao and means to leap or to skip (Strong's G4640). The word joy is translated to the Greek word agalliasis, which means exultation, extreme gladness, the oil of gladness used at feasts *(Strong's G20)*. The unborn baby leaped for joy, and Mary leaped for joy using the element of dance as a form of worship. Following this, Mary sang a prophetic song about who the unborn child was to be and declared purpose to his life as revealed spontaneously in her spirit. Luke 1:44-46 uses the elements of dance, song, and prophecy. Partnering dance with other forms of worship can be used to stir up the prophetic Word of God in the believer. Likewise, other forms of worships can be used to stir up prophetic dance in the believer.

Dance and Singing and Sound

In his sermon, "The Forms of Worship," Ng Waj Lok, says, "There are over 120 references of singing in the Bible. This is the most common form of expression of worship" *(sermoncentral.com)*. *Psalms 100:1, 2, and 4 say, "Make a joyful noise unto the Lord all ye lands. Serve the Lord with gladness: come before his presence with singing.... Enter into His gates with thanksgiving and into his courts with praise".* Noise is translated to the Hebrew word patsach and means to break out in joyful sound, to break forth in joy, to make a loud noise *(Strong's 6476)*. Worshiping God by letting out a shout is acceptable and pleasing to His ears. The term singing in this passage in translated to the Hebrew word renanah, meaning a shout for joy *(Strong's 7445)*. Its root meaning comes from the Hebrew word ranan, meaning to creak, to shout (for joy), to rejoice, to sing, to triumph *(Strong's 7442)*. We are to sing to God because He is triumphant and has made us triumphant. Praise is translated from the Hebrew word tehillah, meaning hymn *(Strong's H8416)*. We are to dance and sing before our Father with a reckless abandonment of self! Psalms 100 combines sound, song, and dance. This combination releases freedom through united worship. With this combination, worshipers are released to be free before God and with each other.

Psalms 33:1-3 says, "Rejoice in the Lord O ye righteous: for praise is comely for the upright. Praise the Lord with harp: sing unto him with psaltery and an instrument of ten strings. Sing unto him a new song; play skillfully with a loud noise".

Rejoice in this passage means to shout, cry out, sing. This passage combines sound, singing, instruments, and dance. *Philippians 4:4 says, "Rejoice in the Lord always and again I say rejoice".* This combination of worship represents the righteousness we have in Christ, and in our righteousness, He causes us to rejoice.

Zechariah 9:9 says, "Rejoice greatly, O daughter of Zion shout, O daughter of Jerusalem: behold, thy King cometh unto thee: he is just, and having salvation... ". Rejoice in this passage is the Hebrew word giyl and means to spin around under the influence of any violent emotion, to be glad, to dance *(Strong's H1523)*. The word shout is translated to the Hebrew word ruwa, meaning to raise a war-cry, or to shout in triumph or distress *(Strong's H7321)*. In this passage, we see a combination of dancing and released sound as forms of worship. In context, this passage is a prophecy of the coming King. Therefore, our dancing and shouting represents the celebration of our returning Savior.

Dance, Flags, and Banners

Psalms 20:5 says, "We will rejoice in thy salvation, and in the name of our God we will set up our banners: the Lord fulfill all thy petitions". The word banners in this passage is the Hebrew word dagal and means to look, behold, carry or set up a banner or standard (in battle). This psalm was written as a prayer of spiritual warfare. Here we see a partnering of movement, banners, and prayer. These elements of worship come together as a weapon in the spirit. *II Corinthians 10:4 says, "The weapons we fight with are not of the world. On the contrary, they have divine power to demolish strongholds"* (NIV). Understanding how various forms of worship come together helps us to be able to effectively do spiritual warfare. Our worship, in all its forms, is our weapon God has given us to use in battle.

Jesus became our banner when He was lifted on the cross. *John 12:32 says, "And I, if I be lifted up from the earth I'll draw all men unto me."* The word lift is the Greek word hupsoo meaning to lift up on high, to exalt, to raise to the summit of opulence and prosperity; to elevate" *(Strong's G5312)*. As we raise our standards in worship, we are exalting Christ, and as we raise our standards in our lives, we are also exalting Christ. He is the standard. *John 3:14 says, "And as Moses lifted up the serpent in the wilderness, even so must the Son of Man be lifted up".*

To worship in unity brings us closer to each other and to God. All worship is beautiful to God and is a reflection of His heart towards us. In her book, Celebration: Banners, Dance, and Holiness in Worship, author Lora Allison states, "When we are in unity we flow in the anointing of God. What else is there? Pride and division stop the flow of that anointing..." *(p.63)*.

We are to bring our gifts together in worship so that we experience the fullness of God's presence. There is not one gift that is more important than another in the Kingdom of God. This is why we are referred to as the body of Christ—because it is our function to live as one with the mindset that we need each other. Working together allows us to reach more and increase our effectiveness over the power of the enemy. God loves worship, and He loves when we worship together on one accord. *Psalms 133:1 says, "Behold, how good and how pleasant it is for brethren to dwell together in unity".* Let there be united worship.

Supernatural Concepts Applied

1. *Ephesians 4 discusses the importance of unity in the faith. What are some ways to stimulate unity among your sphere of influence?*

2. *Beyond the dance, what are some other ways that you can express the messages of the Lord through unity both inside and outside of the local fellowship?*

3. *How can you partner with the other elements in worship to stimulate a culture of the supernatural?*

Chapter Nine

YOU ARE COMMISSIONED!

Then Jesus came to them and said, *"All authority in heaven and on earth has been given to me. Therefore go and make disciples of all nations, baptizing them in the name of the Father and of the Son and of the Holy Spirit, and teaching them to obey everything I have commanded you."* -Matthew 28:18-20

The bigger picture of the Great Commission is that it is how we, as the body of Christ, are to fulfill our purpose to build the Church overall. In order to function in the supernatural, we must understand that we are sent. A commission is an assignment given to a group of people who are officially charged with a particular function. We have been officially charged to carry out the message and mission of Christ who is the One who sends us.

I hear the Lord say, "It's time to operate in the full truth of your function. You must stay connected." God is sending you to the nations. He is sending you to places you cannot even imagine. The dreams you had as a child are coming to pass, but you must remain connected to the Source.

Authority is the power or right to give direction, make decisions, and implement obedience to a vision. Christ is our authority who sends us with His own authority to accompany us. This is why Christ started out with saying where the authority is— in Him. Being one in Him allows us to be sent by Him as our source for the supernatural to function. There are two sources of the supernatural—God or Satan. It is God who gives us power to operate in the supernatural graces. To operate independently of Him opens the door to demonic influence (witchcraft).

He is revealing a spiritual truth. One cannot fully function as a sent one if he/she doesn't remain connected to the one by which he/she was sent.

The Bible states in *John 15:4-5, "Abide in Me, and I in you. As the branch cannot bear fruit of itself unless it abides in the vine, so neither can you unless you abide in Me. I am the vine, you are the branches; he who abides in Me and I in him, he bears much fruit, for apart from Me you can do nothing".*

Typically, people focus on the bearing fruit part of that passage. But the key is in the abiding. We can't do do anything without the power and presence of Christ. To abide means to stay or remain. This requires consecration as a lifestyle. We are in a time where we must be relentless about functioning as Kingdom citizens. We have to function according to the statutes of our Kingdom, not the kingdom of this world. We have to adopt heaven on earth as our mentality.

Jesus told us to pray, *"So then, this is how you should pray: 'Our Father in heaven, hallowed be Your name, Your Kingdom come, Your will be done, on earth as it is in Heaven"* (*Matthew 6:9,10*).

The word kingdom in this passage means to have sovereign rule, or authority over someone or something. In order to have a postured revelation of the supernatural one must first understand the kingdom authority established and extended to the body of Christ (the ekklesia) in and through the triune God. Our kingdom authority comes from the power of the King. Which was extended to us through Christ. His power is revealed in and through us by the Holy Spirit.

Many default and limit the in-working of the Holy Spirit to the speaking of the tongues. *Acts 2:4 says, "And they were all filled with the Holy Ghost, and began to speak with other tongues, as the Spirit gave them utterance.* "What is described in this passage is the infilling of the Holy Spirit- or the baptism of the Holy Spirit. This is only the beginning. Once the Holy Spirit comes alive in us, we are endowed with power to function by the power of the Holy Spirit. The Lord says, "Now when you dance, go forth in POWER!"

God gave us the Holy Spirit to accompany us as we tell of His greatness, and mercy. In this regard the Holy Spirit serves as our witness that God is truth. That Christ truly is the way. This power is not to be done in our own might, but by the Spirit of God.

Please note that the supernatural realm is independent of anything of self, and cannot be comprehended by the natural mind. Functioning in the supernatural can only occur by yielding to the Holy Spirit. *Romans 8:14 says, "For as many as are led by the Spirit of God, they are the sons of God."* We must be very sensitive to the leading of the Holy Spirit as to when and how He wants us to move.

Jesus Christ is the only way into the Kingdom of Heaven. In the time that we are in, there are people who cannot hear the message of the gospel because their hearts are hardened. We must go back to the original principles and patterns of the Bible. It is God's will that we operate as virtuous citizens in the kingdom. To have virtue means to have high moral standards, and also means to have integrity, dignity, honor, respectability, and purity. These are all attributes of God and are reflected in how we care for and function in the Holy Spirit. God has given us virtue to be able to execute the Kingdom in the Earth.

Go In Power and the Might of the Lord

I Corinthians 2:4 says, "And my speech and my preaching was not with enticing. Many people are like Moses crying, "Show me your glory," but God is saying, "My glory is within you! Believe again and reveal my glory to others." People not only want to hear what we have to say; they want to see if what we say is real.

This was God's purpose for making us His ambassadors—to reveal who He is in the earth. An ambassador is one who is sent to serve as an official representative. As we are sent to serve in the dances of the supernatural, we are to represent the Kingdom.

It is my prayer that the dance will be transformed so that we will go forth in the power and might of the Lord to represent to Kingdom in wisdom, grace, and love.

WORKS CITED

Arnold, Kina N. "The Priesthood of the Dance: A Manual for the Sacred Dancer Revised Edition," Nobody But God Printing and Publishing Services, Inc., [...], Print.

Ashby, William Brent & Galan, Benjamin. "The Rose Guide to the Tabernacle," Rose Publishing, 2008. Print

Brickner, David, "Finding Jesus in the Feast of Tabernacles," CBN. com, 2014. Website.

Clark, Heather, "DANCE as the Spirit Moves," Destiny Image Publishing, 2009. Print.

Conner, Kevin J. "The Tabernacle of David," City Christian Publishing, 1976. Print

Conner, Kevin J. "The Tabernacle of Moses," City Christian Publishing, 1976. Print

Curry, Karen M. "Dancing In the Spirit: Scriptural Study of Liturgical Dance," Author House, 2004. Print.

Dankenburg, William F. "A New Look at the Deep Meaning of the Feast of Tabernacles," hope-of-israel.org, Triumph Prophetic Ministries, 2014. Website, eBook.

Dr. Hardy, Pamela. "Let the Nations Rejoice!" Books Writers Agency, 2011. Print.

Dr. Hardy, Pamela. "Make His Praise Glorious," [....], Print.

Eymann, Julie. "The Biblical Significance of Dance," [....], Article.

Ezell, Rick. "Committing Your All to Jesus- Romans 12," Lifeway Ministries, 2012. Article.

Got Questions Ministries, "What is the Feast of Weeks," gotquestions. org, 2002-2014. Website.

Gordon, I. "Jesus in the Tabernacle: An Introduction and Overview of the Tabernacle," jesusplusnothing.com. [...]. Article.

Slemming, C. W. "These are the Garments," CLC Publications, 2012. Print.

Sorge, Bob. "Exploring Worship: A Practical Guide to Praise and Worship," Oasis House, 1987, 2001. Print

Strong, James H. Strong's Exhaustive Concordance Complete and Unabridged, Baker Book House, 1985. Print.

Zondervan. "Life in the Spirit Study Bible King James Version," 1992. Print.

WEBSITES AND REFERENCES
www.biblegateway.com
www.bible-history.com
www.biblehub.org
www.blueletterbible.org
www.dictionary.com
www.google.com
www.kingjamesbibleonline.org
www.watchmanforjesus.blogspot.com
www.wikipedia.org

Made in the USA
Lexington, KY
21 September 2019